The Wizards Cookbook

Discover the 100 Magic Recipes inspired by Harry Potter
and become the protagonist by recreating the sweet
and savory dishes from the series.

Steve Bellaria

Table of Contents

INTRODUCTION

The Wizards Cookbook includes recipes inspired by the fantasy, imagination, and characters created by J.K. Rowling in her books and film adaptations. Each recipe is prepared with the utmost reverence for the series's spirit through combining flavors, cooking methods, and ingredients that J.K. herself might have detailed in one of her books.

The book contains magical recipes. Each recipe features a page of compelling stories that delve into how that dish was served, the occasion in which the characters were served the dish, and what each dish contributed to the plot.

This cookbook is the best present for any foodie Potter-fan and the ideal companion on a train trip to Hogwarts. It might help, too, to get into the minds and hearts of the characters. Or maybe you'll like to make some yummy food and read a few good stories at the same time.

This book is a collection of recipes I've learned, created, or combined to recreate meals from the series, including specialties from the great and small wizarding establishments of the Wizarding World. Every recipe in this book has a gripping story beside it.

This cookbook is intended for magical purposes only. Though some of the ingredients and techniques might be suitable for everyday cooking, that isn't the point. The point is that you should throw caution to the wind, be full of wonder and magic, and play with ingredients and spices without a great deal of an idea how you are going to use them and create unique dishes you'll remember for the rest of your life.

Even when the series stopped, the magic in our hearts has been living forever. If you have grown up with Harry and his friends, fighting each battle and living every laughter, these recipes will surely make you go home to Hogwarts once again.

Anyway, even non-wizard folk can conjure up something wonderful and delicious in an instant with this book. Instead of waving a wand, you will be equipped with choice kitchen utensils and some powerful recipes. These pages are the secret to conjuring up delicious treats, wonderful dishes, and delectable potions, plus so much more. For anyone not familiar with British cuisine, foods in the young wizard series may seem just that, foreign, but it plays an important part in the U.K. island culture with a rich historical past and fascinating beginnings.

Join us on an adventure to enjoy these perfect recipes that are sure to lift your spirits and make you reminiscent of the Wizarding world once again.

With our one hundred carefully handpicked delicacies, you know you are in for a ride to the Whomping Willow from the cozy Burrow. This book is a selection of the yummiest and magical feasts that you could ever want. Are you planning on a Harry Potter-themed Birthday Bash, party, or just a home affair? Show off your cooking magic at the next event and get them talking about it for weeks?

LET'S COOK!

CHAPTER 1: SAVORY RECIPES

1. Roast Beef

Roast beef in the Great Hall was a staple whenever there was a storm outside. Dumbledore ensured that the students felt comfort from the hailing winds outside with the warmth and coziness of the classic Roast Beef. You don't need the skills of a house-elf to make delicious roast beef.

Yield: 6 to 7 servings
Prep time: 2 hours and 20 minutes
Cook time: 3 hours; 30 minutes to rest

Ingredients:
• 3 to 3 ½ pounds round roast
• 3 or 4 cloves garlic, slivered
• olive oil
• salt
• ground pepper
• dried rosemary
• dried thyme
• dried parsley

Instructions:
1. Let the round roast sit at room temperature for 2 hours to help it cook evenly.
2. Once the meat has evenly warmed, preheat the oven to 365°F.
3. Remove the wrapping from the meat and thoroughly rinse.
4. Pat the roast dry with paper towels and set it on a plate.
5. Using a knife, slit several holes around the roast. Place slivers of garlic into each incision.
6. Brush olive oil over the whole roast.
7. Sprinkle the salt, pepper, rosemary, thyme, and parsley over the roast.

8. Position a rimmed baking sheet or pan under the lower rack of your oven. The pan will catch the drippings from the roast.
9. Place the roast directly on the lower rack, fat-side up, over the pan.
10. Roast for 3 hours.
11. When the internal temperature is between 135°F and 140°F, the roast is ready. Now remove it from the oven and place it on a cutting board.
12. Tenting with aluminum foil over the meat and let it rest for 30 minutes before carving. This helps to seal in the juices.
13. Thinly slice the meat and serve.

<u>2. Bacon-Wrapped Sausage Bites</u>

Even the Yule Ball tables were full of dishes with these favorites. These are an easy yet extremely satisfying side dish or appetizer for any grand meal.

Yield: 10 to 15 servings
Prep time: 7 to 10 minutes
Cook time: 30 to 40 minutes

Ingredients:
• brown sugar
• 1 pound thick-cut bacon, halved lengthwise
• 7 ounces cocktail sausages

Instructions:
1. Preheat the oven to 400°F.
2. Put the aluminum foil on a sheet pan and cover with brown sugar.
3. Wrap the narrow strips of bacon around the sausages and place them on the pan.
4. Sprinkle more brown sugar over the meat.
5. Bake until the bacon is crisp (35-40 min).

3. Baked Pumpkin

This recipe is quick and easy: cut up your pumpkin (save the seeds for later toasting), spice it up, and put it in the oven to roast. You'll have a delicious fall dish in no time.

Yield: 4 servings
Prep time: 5 minutes
Cook time: 20 minutes

Ingredients:
• 1 small pumpkin or ¼ of a giant pumpkin, seeded and sliced in 1-inch-thick slices
• 2 tablespoons olive oil
• pinch of ground clove
• 1 teaspoon ground cinnamon
• ¼ teaspoon ground nutmeg
• 1 teaspoon sea salt
• 2 tablespoons packed brown sugar
• feta, seeds, and chopped parsley, for topping (optional)

Instructions:
1. Preheat the oven to 400°F.
2. Put the pumpkin slices on a baking sheet. Drizzle the olive oil over the pumpkin and use a pastry brush to cover the pieces with oil.
3. Sprinkle with the seasonings and the sugar on the slices.
4. Put the sheet in the oven and bake for 20 minutes or until the edges begin to become golden brown.
5. Pick it from the oven and let it cool for some minutes.

4. Chipolatas

Chipolatas are a staple of an English Christmas dinner, no matter if it's a wizarding or a non-magical feast. This recipe includes a few extra ingredients along with the sausages to pack in more flavor. The only consolation Ron had after Fleur turned him down for the Yule Ball were these delicious delicacies.

Yield: 6 servings
Prep time: 10 minutes; 2 hours to marinate
Cook time: 30 to 40 minutes

Ingredients:
- 10 to 12 ounces cocktail sausages
- 4 strips uncooked bacon, cut to bits
- 4 ½ tablespoons maple syrup
- ¼ cup pineapple juice
- ¼ cup pineapple chunks

Instructions:
1. Place all of the ingredients in an oven-safe pan.
2. Cover the pan with foil and marinate for 2 hours.
3. Preheat the oven to 400°F.
4. Then uncover the pan to place it in the oven and bake for 30 to 40 minutes or until the bacon crisps.
5. Then remove the pan and let the sausages cool for 1 to 2 minutes.
6. Serve hot.

5. Goulash

The stands in the Quidditch World Cup served this to everyone for free the first day to warm them up before the match.

Yield: 6 servings
Prep time: 10 minutes
Cook time: 30 minutes

Ingredients:
• 1 pound ground turkey
• 2 medium onions, chopped
• 4 cloves garlic, chopped
• 4 large carrots, chopped
• 1 teaspoon plus one dash of salt, divided
• 8 ounces macaroni
• 1 (14.5-ounce) can crushed tomatoes
• 1 (14.5-ounce) can diced tomatoes
• ½ teaspoon ground pepper
• 3 or 4 stems fresh parsley, chopped, plus more for garnish
• 2 teaspoons dried basil
• 3 teaspoons dried oregano
• 1 bell pepper (any color), chopped

Instructions:
1. Preheat a cast-iron skillet on the stovetop over medium heat. Once the pan is heated, add the ground turkey.
2. Brown the meat for 5 to 7 minutes and drain the fat.
3. Place the pan with the meat back on the stove, and add the onions, garlic, carrots, and salt teaspoon. Cook for 5-7 minutes.
4. Fill a large saucepot with water and add a dash of salt. Bring the water to a boil.

5. Reduce the heat under the meat to low, and cover the pan with a lid while the water is boiling.

6. Put the macaroni in the water, then cook to al dente. Remove the pasta from the heat and drain. Return the pasta to the saucepot over low heat.

7. Add the meat mixture to the saucepot with the noodles.

8. Add to the pot the smashed tomatoes and the sliced tomatoes.

9. Add the pepper and dried herbs, stirring until they are thoroughly incorporated.

10. Add the bell pepper.

11. Simmer over low heat for 5 minutes.

12. Garnish with fresh parsley and serve immediately.

6. Dainty Tea Sandwiches

These are four different tea sandwiches that cater to almost everyone.

Yield: 3 sandwiches per 2 slices of bread
Prep time: 2/3 minutes per sandwich

Ingredients:
• Ham and Cheese
• soft wheat, honey wheat, or similar "light" flavored bread
• sliced deli ham
• sliced Swiss cheese or one large wedge of Brie
• butter (omit with Brie)
• Cream Cheese and Cucumber
• soft wheat, honey wheat, or similar "light" flavored bread
 • 1 medium cucumber
• cream cheese softened
• handful of fresh cilantro leaves
• dried oregano

- Smoked Salmon and Cream Cheese
- soft wheat, honey wheat, or similar "light" flavored bread
- smoked salmon
- cream cheese softened
- Pepperoni and Cream Cheese
- soft wheat, honey wheat, or similar "light" flavored bread
- pepperoni slices
- cream cheese softened
- dash of thyme, rosemary, and ground black pepper

Instructions:
1. Spread a thin to moderate layer of cream cheese or butter on one side of the two slices of bread for each sandwich. For the ham and Brie, spread the Brie.
2. Layer on the meat, fish, or vegetable ingredients thickly. This is especially important for the pepperoni and the salmon.
3. Layer on any cheese toppings in a single-slice layer.
4. Add any additional ingredients in a thin layer on top of the ingredients or sprinkle seasoning over the other ingredients.
5. Top with closing bread slice.
6. Cut off the crusts of the sandwiches and cut each into three sections.
7. Serve immediately for the freshest flavor.

7. Fiery Flobberworms

Fiery flobberworms are made of boneless flobberworms coated in a savory, crunchy paste.

Serves: 3-4
Preparation Time: 30 minutes
Cooking Time: 10 minutes

Ingredients:
• Fish or chicken 1 lb. 2 oz. (boneless fillets)
• All-purpose flour 1 cup
• Salt to taste
• Red chili powder (optional) to taste
• Black Pepper powder ½ tsp. or to taste
• Garlic paste ½ tsp.
• Cumin powder 1 tsp.
• Egg 1 (beaten)
• Lemon juice 2 tbsp.
• Water ½ cup
• Bread crumbs 1 ½ cup
• Oil as needed (for frying)

Instructions:
1. Mix the flour, salt, red chili powder, black pepper powder, garlic paste, cumin powder, egg, lemon juice, and water in a bowl.
2. Marinate the fish/chicken fillet in the mixture for around 30 minutes.
3. Layout the bread crumbs in a shallow dish for easy use.
4. Heat the oil in a deep frying pan. Coat each fillet lavishly with bread crumbs and add them to the frying pan. Turn them occasionally and fry until the fillets turn golden.
5. Once cooked, take the fillets out and drain them on a kitchen towel.
6. Serve hot with French fries.

8. Roast Potatoes

Harry was delighted by how many dishes come out of nowhere during his first feast at Hogwarts. There were lots of enticing dishes to chose from, including roast potatoes. Maybe he helped himself with those roast potatoes again and again, and that's what we're going to do with this dumb recipe!

Serves: 4-6
Preparation Time: 10-15 minutes

Ingredients:
- Potatoes 2.5 lbs.
- Duck fat 5 tbsp.
- All-purpose flour 2 tbsp.
- Salt to taste
- Oregano/thyme 1 tsp.

Instructions:
1. Parboil the potatoes for 6-7 minutes until they are almost cooked. Don't overdo them if you want crispy potatoes. They should be firm from the outside. Drain them using a colander.
2. Preheat the oven to 350 °F.
3. Now, place the duck fat in a roasting pan; put it in the oven for a minute or two.
4. When the duck fat melts, add the drained potatoes to it. Add the oregano and thyme and roll the potatoes so they are evenly coated with grease.
5. Place the baking sheet in the oven; fry for 40-50 minutes. Cook until they are golden brown.

9. Meat Balls

Molly Weasley was famous for her mouthwatering meatballs. Would you like some Molly-ish Meatballs?

Serves: 6
Preparation Time: 20 minutes
Cooking Time: 30 minutes

Ingredients:

For Meatballs:
• Onions 2 large (finely chopped)
• Fresh Rosemary 2 tbsp.
• Olive oil 3 tbsp.
• Worcestershire Sauce 2 tbsp.
 • Garlic 1 clove (crushed)
• Minced Beef 2 lbs.
• Bread crumbs ½ cup
• Cheddar cheese 2 oz.
• Ground salt and pepper to taste

For Sauce:
• Olive Oil 2 tbsp.
• Onion 1 medium-sized (sliced)
• Tomato cans 2 x 14 oz.

Instructions:
1. Pour 1 tbsp. oil in a pan; now, fry the chopped onions and rosemary leaves until the onions are light pink. Add the Worcestershire sauce and a little water and cook for 10 minutes or until the water disappears. Leave to cool.

2. Take a bowl in which you can mix the ground meat, salt, pepper, garlic, bread crumbs, and onions.

3. Divide and form equal-sized meatballs.

4. Poke some cheese into the center of each ball. Roll and perfect your meatballs. Refrigerate or freeze until required.

5. Heat oil in a pan.

6. Toss in the onion and fry until it is lightly golden.

7. Now add the tomatoes and some water (if required) and season according to taste with herbs and spices.

8. Cook the tomatoes until they are softened.

9. Preheat the oven to 475 °F and the oven-proof dish.

10. Put the rest of the oil in the oven-proof dish and place the meatballs in it. Cook for 10-15 minutes.

11. Take the pan out and pour in the gravy. Now let it cook for another 3-4 minutes in the oven.

12. Serve with mashed potatoes or spaghetti.

10. Molly's Meatballs and Onion Sauce

Serving Size: 4
Prep time: 10 minutes
Total Prep time: 35 minutes

Ingredients:

Meatballs
• ½ cup fresh or dry breadcrumbs
• 1 lb. extra-lean ground beef
• 1 onion, finely chopped
• 1 large egg
• 2 Tbsp. vegetable oil

- 2 Tbsp. chopped fresh parsley
- 1 clove garlic, crushed
- ½ tsp. salt
- 1 tsp. Worcestershire sauce
- 1/8 tsp. nutmeg
- ¼ tsp. freshly ground black pepper

Onion Sauce
- 2 Tbsp. vegetable oil
- 1 onion, chopped
- 1 Tbsp. all-purpose flour
- 1 (14-oz) can chicken broth
- 1 tsp. Worcestershire sauce
- 1 bay leaf

Instructions:
1. Combine all the meatballs ingredients in a bowl.
2. Make 1.5-inch small meatballs out of this mixture.
3. Heat oil in a pan. Sear the meatballs for 4 minutes side.
4. Sauté onion in a greased skillet until golden brown.
5. Add flour and stir cook for 1 minute.
6. Pour in broth, Worcestershire sauce, and bay leaf.
7. Stir cook until it thickens.
8. Put the meatballs in the sauce, then cook for 15 minutes.
9. Serve with egg noodles.

11. Mashed Potatoes

Yield: 6 servings
Prep time: 15 minutes
Cook time: 20 minutes

Ingredients:
- 2 pounds russet potatoes, peeled and chopped
- 1 cup milk
- Two tablespoons butter
- ½ teaspoon Italian seasoning
- ½ teaspoon parsley flakes
- ½ teaspoon salt
- ½ teaspoon freshly ground black pepper
- ½ teaspoon minced onion
- ½ teaspoon garlic powder
- ½ teaspoon dried cilantro

Instructions:
1. In a large saucepot, bring water with a pinch of salt to a boil.
2. Once the water is boiling, place the potatoes in the water and cook for 15 minutes or until tender.
3. Carefully drain the potatoes and return them to the saucepot.
4. Add the milk and butter to a small saucepan over medium-low heat. Stir until the butter melts.
5. Bring the milk and butter mix to a boil, occasionally stirring to prevent burning.
6. While you are waiting for the milk and butter mix to boil, use a large fork or potato masher to mash it.
7. Once the butter and milk mix boils, remove it from the heat.
8. Gently stir the milk and butter mixture into the mashed potatoes until the potatoes become creamy.

9. Work the potatoes with a large fork until they become fluffy.
10.   Thoroughly blend in the spices.
11.   Serve hot.

12. Sorting Hat Cheese Balls

Servings: 30
Prep Time: 3 hours and 30 minutes

Ingredients:
- 2 (8 oz) packages cream cheese, softened
- 1/2 cup (1 stick) butter, softened
- 2.5 cups shredded cheddar cheese
- 1 (0.7 oz) package Italian salad dressing mix
- ¼ cup poppy seeds
- Veggies or crackers

Instructions:
1. Combine the cream cheese, butter, cheese, and dressing mix in a stand mixer and mix on medium until well combined.
2. Shape a third of the cheese mixture into a six-inch diameter disc shape to create the brim of the hat.
3. Form the rest of the cheese mixture into a cone shape. This will be the top part of the hat.
4. Cover both shapes in plastic wrap, then place it into the fridge for at least one hour.
5. Take the shapes out of the fridge, place the cone on top of the disc, put it on top of the disc on your serving platter, and blend them. Shape the facial features into the cone and bend the point back slightly to define the sorting hat in a bit more detail.

6. Press the poppy seeds into the surface of the cheese hat until you have completely covered it. The easiest way to do this is by sprinkling the seeds into your palms and gently pressing them on the larger sections. This will get a little messy, so to avoid a tedious cleanup, place a cloth underneath it.
7. Gently wrap the plastic wrap around the cheese ball hat and place it into the refrigerator for at least two hours. Do this the day before and leave it overnight.
8. Take it out of the fridge thirty minutes before serving with your favorite vegetables or crackers.

13. Sun-Dried Tomato and Basil Sorting Hat Rolls

Servings: 16
Prep Time: 25 minutes
Cook Time: 10-15 minutes

Ingredients:
- Two tubes (8 oz each) refrigerated crescent rolls
- ¼ cup butter softened
- ¼ cup minced fresh basil
- 2 tbsp oil-packed sun-dried tomatoes, patted dry and finely chopped
- ½ tsp garlic powder

Instructions:
1. Preheat the oven to 375 degrees F.
2. Unroll each of the tubes of dough and separate each dough roll into eight triangles.
3. Using a small bowl, mix the garlic powder, sun-dried tomatoes, basil, and softened butter.

4. Spread a teaspoon of the filling along the wide end of each of the triangles and carefully roll up each triangle once to form the hat's brim.
5. Place the triangles separately on a greased baking sheet and bake for ten to twelve minutes or until they turn golden brown. Turn them halfway to brown evenly.

14. Hundred Layer Chicken & Ham Sandwich

Servings: 10-12
Prep Time: 20-30 minutes
Cook Time: 5-10 minutes

Ingredients:
- Two red onions
- 1 tbsp oil
- pinch salt
- pepper (to taste)
- 2 tbsp brown sugar
- 1/2 tbsp balsamic vinegar
- 5 tbsp mayonnaise
- 1/2 tbsp wholegrain mustard
- 2 oz margarine/butter
- One small lettuce
- Six tomatoes
- 20-30 slices of chicken
- 20-30 slices of ham
- skewers (for support)
- white bread

Instructions:
1. Cut and slice onions into thin rings. Heat a pan with oil in it and add the onions, stirring it for 5 minutes until they start turning golden. Use

salt and pepper to season and add in the balsamic vinegar and sugar, stirring for 2-3 minutes until the sauce thickens. Move from the pan into a bowl and let it cool.
2. Then add the mayonnaise and mustard into a bowl and mix them until combined.
3. Wash and rinse your tomatoes and lettuce, and then slice them both into thin rounds and shreds.
4. Now layout bread and begin to stack the layers, starting with bread and butter and alternating each layer with filling and additional bread slices, using the skewers to keep the layers from collapsing until you reach your goal. Don't rush the process. Take your time and steady the sandwich as you go.

15. Cursed Chicken Nuggets

Servings: 25 -28
Prep Time: 15 minutes
Cook Time: 15 minutes

Ingredients:
- 1 pound ground chicken
- One teaspoon garlic powder
- One teaspoon onion powder
- 2 cups bread crumbs

Instructions:
1. Preheat the oven to 350 degrees F.
2. Line a baking tray with parchment paper.
3. Spread breadcrumbs on a plate to dip in the shaped chicken nuggets.
4. Add the ground chicken into a large bowl.
5. Add your seasonings and stir to combine. The seasoning can also be switched up or kept the same for taste.

6. To create the shape, roll out a log shape from the mixture and coat it in breadcrumbs. Lay the covered log on some parchment paper and shape it into the lightning scar. Shaping is easier once the mixture has been coated in breadcrumbs.
7. To make the glasses, repeat the same steps as above, but when shaping the glasses, make two circles and connect them in the center with a small nose-bridge and put it all together on the parchment paper.
8. Repeat before all the chicken has been used.
9. Bake for 20 minutes at 350 degrees F. Thinner parts may take less time to cook. Shapes may take a bit longer to cook.

16. Simple Meat Pies

Preparation time: 20min
Cooking time: 15min
Servings: 4

Ingredients:
- 1 lb. Chuck Beef, finely diced but not minced
- 1 turnip or swede, chopped
- one potato, diced
- Two onions, chopped
- ½ cup of Tomato Sauce
- ¼ cup of Worcestershire Sauce Black pepper and salt to taste 1 lb. Croissant dough
- 1 egg + 1 tsp. water, beaten

Instructions:
1. Combine the ingredients in a bowl (except the dough). Let it marinate for about 30 minutes.
2. Then separate the dough into four parts. Roll out into circles.

3. Fill each with about 3 tbsp of the meat mixture.
4. Water the edges, close them, and press them with a fork or make a curve.
5. Place the pies on a cooking sheet tray lined with parchment paper. Pierce the dough and brush with beaten eggs.
6. Bake for 15min at 375F (preheated oven).

17. Hogsmeade Chicken Spindles

Ingredients:
- 8 chicken spindles
- 50 g of butter
- 70 g of breadcrumbs
- 1 tablespoon of honey
- 1 tablespoon of soy sauce
- Salt

Instructions:
1. Place the chicken spindles in a bowl, pour the soy sauce and honey, then mix and leave to marinate for at least 2 hours.
2. Drain the chicken drumsticks from the marinade and add salt.
3. Melt the butter and brush the spindles well.
4. Pass the buttered chicken drumsticks in the grated breadcrumbs.
5. Line a baking tray with parchment paper, place the spindles on top and cook them at 200 ° C for 30-40 minutes.
6. Serve the spindles hot.

18. Irish Soda Bread

Mrs. Weasley always seems to know what kind of food will hit the spot, regardless of the time of day. She is most famous for preparing fresh homemade bread such as this dish.

Cooking Time: 1 hour
Serving: 8

Ingredients:
- 4 cups all-purpose flour, extra for dusting
- 1 ½ teaspoon baking soda
- 1 ½ teaspoon of cream of tartar
- 1 teaspoon of salt
- 3 tablespoons of white sugar
- 4 tablespoons of butter
- 1 egg, beaten
- 1 ½ cups of buttermilk

Instructions:
1. Preheat the oven to 425 degrees. In a round baking dish, grease with cooking spray and dust lightly with flour.
2. In a bowl, add in the all-purpose flour, cream of tartar, a dash of salt, white sugar, and baking soda. Stir well to mix. Add in the butter and cut in with a pastry cutter until crumbly inconsistency.
3. Add in the egg and buttermilk. Stir well until a dough forms.
4. Put the kneading on a floured surface and knead it for 2-3 minutes. Shape into a round and put in a greased bowl. Dust the end of the flour dough. Slice and X at the tip of the dough.
5. Place in the oven and bake for 15 minutes. Lower the oven heat to 350 degrees.
6. Now, after remove, set onto a wire rack to cool completely.
7. Serve.

19. Popcorn Balls

Time: 30 Minutes
Servings: 4

Ingredients:
- 60 gr (4 tbsp) of butter
- 1 kg (4 cups) marshmallows (miniature)
- 1 bag of popcorn
- 1 teaspoon vanilla extract
- 1/4 teaspoon salt
- 350 gr (1 and ½ cups) of candy corn

Instructions:
1. Prepare a baking sheet with aluminum foil. Sprinkle the foil with a non-stick cooking spray.
2. Place the popcorn and candy corn in a large bowl and set them aside.
3. Put the butter in a microwave for 30-45 seconds to melt it. Add the marshmallows and microwave for another 90 seconds to melt them. The marshmallows may not seem to melt, but once you mix them, they should liquefy.
4. Stir to melt the butter and marshmallows, then add the vanilla and salt and mix until the candies are well mixed.
5. Pour the marshmallow mixture over the popcorn and candy corns and mix until combined. Leave the mixture to rest for a few minutes to cool the hot marshmallow.
6. Use a non a non-stick cooking spray on your hands and collect a handful of popcorn. Press firmly between your hands, forming a ball shape. Make sure the balls are compact; loosely formed popcorn balls come off easily.
7. If the balls don't form, let the mixture sit for another minute.

8. Place the popcorn balls on the pan. Let them solidify at room temperature.
9. Store the popcorn balls in a cool, dry room.

20. Hogwarts House Cup Chicken

It has basic seasoning, including garlic, onion powder, salt, and pepper. Honey and lemon juice add a sweet juicy feel to every bite.

Prep Time: 10 minutes
Total Prep Time: 20 minutes
Serving: 12

Ingredients:
• 12 chicken drumsticks
• 2 tsp. dried basil
• Garlic powder, to taste
• Onion powder, to taste
• Salt, to taste
• Black pepper, to taste
• 2 Tbsp. honey

Instructions:
1. Rub the drumsticks with salt, olive oil, pepper, onion powder, and garlic powder.
2. Arrange the drumsticks on a baking sheet in a single layer.
3. Sprinkle dried basil on top.
4. Mix honey with lemon juice and pour over the chicken.
5. Bake for 20 minutes at 375 degrees.
6. Rotate the drumsticks and bake for 20 minutes.
7. Serve warm.

21. Bertie Bott's Every Flavor Beans

These every flavor beans are the particular item at Honeydukes Sweetshop. Dumbledore presented Harry, Ron, and Hermione with a huge amount of these magical beans. We created our version because, according to Dumbledore, every flavor may end up in some disgusting one too. So, staying on the safe side here is a special recipe for all of these flavor beans.

Serving size: 10
Cooking time: 1 hour 50 minutes

Ingredients:
- Chopped bacon – 6 slices
- Ground beef – 1 pound
- Baked beans with pork – 2 cans
- Navy beans – 1 can
- Kidney beans – 1 can
- Ketchup – ¾ cup
- Brown sugar – ¾ cup
- White vinegar (distilled) – 3 tbsp
- Onion powder – 1 tsp
- Honey garlic sauce – 2 tbsp
- Garlic salt – 1 tsp
- Worcestershire sauce – 1 tsp
- Ground Mustard – 1 tsp
- Sweet and sour sauce – 2 tbsp

Instructions:
1. Fry the pieces of bacon in a skillet until crisp and brown. Remove pan and set it aside.

2. Crush the beef into the pan. Stir while cooking until the color is changed. Drain off grease and transfer bacon and beef into a cooker.
3. Pour the Ketchup, vinegar, brown sugar, kidney beans, navy beans, and baked
4. beans into the slow cooker. Add sweet and sour sauce, honey garlic sauce, mustard powder, Worcestershire sauce, garlic salt, and onion powder into it.
5. Keep stirring until everything is evenly distributed.
6. Cover with lid and cook for an hour on high heat before serving.

22. Mrs. Weasley's corn beef sandwich

Serving size: 15
Cooking time: 4 hours

Ingredients:
- Corned beef briskets – 3 lb. (with spice packets)
- Beer bottles – 2
- Bay leaves – 2
- Peppercorns – ¼ cup
- Garlic cloves (peeled) – 1 bulb

Instructions:
1. Put corned beef briskets in a large pot—dust only one spice packet. Pour beer and fill a pot with water so much that briskets are covered by 1 inch.
2. Now, add peppercorns, garlic cloves, and bay leaves. Cover with a lid and bring to boil.

3. When a boil comes, bring the heat to low and let it simmer for 4 hours. Keep checking on an hourly basis and add some more water if required to cover the meat.
4. After that, remove meat from the container. Set meat on the cutting board and allow it to firm up a little for 10 minutes. Shred or slice to serve. Discard the liquid of cooking.
5. You can add any vegetables you like.

23. Quidditch World Cup Pasties

The 422nd Quidditch World Cup was a mega event in the fourth book of the series "Harry Potter and the Goblet of Fire." Since it was taking place in England, wizards and witches from across the globe enjoyed local foods. Pasties were the most prominent among those foods. Make pasties with our version and let your brain take you to the biggest sports extravaganza of the Potter World.

Serving size: 4
Cooking time: 1 hour

Ingredients*:
- Baking potatoes (peeled and sliced) – 5
- Chopped onion – 1
- Diced rutabaga – 1 cup
- Chopped pork – 1 lb.
- Butter – ¼ cup
- Recipe Pastry for a 9-inch double-crust pie – 1
- Salt, pepper – To taste
- Garlic cloves (crushed) - 2

Instructions:
1. Preheat the oven to 400 F.
2. Roll the dough to make four thin circles.
3. Place onion over half portion of every circle, potatoes, pork, and rutabaga in an order. Add butter and sprinkle pepper and salt according to your taste. Add garlic (crushed).
4. Fold the dough over the filling and roll, and pinch on the edges. Make few holes with a fork on top and place them on a cookie sheet. Bake in the oven for 45 minutes or until golden brown.

24. Bouillabaisse

Hermione is a "mudblood" or "muggle-born" witch. It means her parents were common human beings without any magical powers. She is the wisest witch of all time, and her brains save Harry and Ron uncountable times from disasters. She likes to savor this French dish. Here is our version of Bouillabaisse.

Serving size: 12
Cooking time: 40 minutes

Ingredients:
- Thinly sliced onions – 2
- Sliced leeks – 2
- Peeled and chopped tomatoes – 3
- Minced garlic cloves – 4
- Olive oil – ¾ cup Bay leaf -1
- Sprig fresh thyme – 1
- Sprig fennel leaf – 1

- Cleaned and debearded mussels – ¾ lb.
- Orange zest – 1tsp
- Sea bass – 5 lb.
- Boiling water – 9 cups
- Saffron threads – 1 pinch
- Fresh shrimp (peeled and deveined) - ¾ lb.
- Salt and pepper - To taste

Instructions:

1. In a saucepan, heat olive oil and add leeks, garlic, chopped tomatoes, and onions. Stir and cook on low flame until vegetables become soft.
2. Add thyme, orange zest, bay leaf, and fennel and stir. Now, add boiling water and shellfish and stir. Sprinkle pepper and salt to taste.
3. Boil for 3 minutes on high heat to let water and oil combine.
4. Reduce heat to low and add fish. Keep cooking for 25 minutes or until the fish is done. The fish needs to be tender and opaque but not falling apart.
5. Check the taste and adjust seasoning if needed.
6. Add saffron and stir. Then pour Bouillabaisse into soup dishes and enjoy.

25. Lamb stew

Leaky Cauldron is an exclusive eatery for the people of the magical world in the Harry Potter series. Along with many others, this lamb stew is also their specialty. If you are on holiday and want to have a real feel of the harry potter series, try this yummy stew.

Serving size: 12
Cooking time: 1 hour 30 minutes

Ingredients:

- Olive oil – 3 tbsp
- Large chopped onion – 1
- Lamb shoulder (sliced in 2-inch pieces) – 3 lb.
- Chopped celery – 1 stalk
- Tomato sauce – 1 can
- Hot water – 3 cups
- Dried mint – ½ tsp
- Dried dill weed – ½ tsp
- White sugar – 1 pinch
- ground cinnamon – 1 pinch
- Trimmed green beans – 2 lb.
- Fresh parsley (chopped) – 1 tbsp
- Pepper – To taste
- Salt - To taste

Instructions:

1. Heat the oil in a big pot. Sauté celery and onion until golden.
2. Stir in the lamb. Cook until it is evenly brown. Add water and tomato sauce and stir.
3. Reduce heat; let it cook for an hour.
4. Add the green beans. Then, add dill weed, mint, parsley, pepper, salt, sugar, and cinnamon. Keep cooking until beans become tender.
5. Serve hot.

26. Lamb chops

Leaky Cauldron is an exclusive eatery for the people of the magical world in the Harry Potter series. Along with many others, this lamb stew is also their specialty. If you are on holiday and want to have a real feel of the Harry Potter series, try this yummy stew to complement your book.

Serving size: 10
Cooking time: 25 minutes

Ingredients:
- Lamb chops – 10
- Minced garlic cloves – 8
- Olive oil – ¼ cup
- Ground black pepper – two tsp
- Minced Ginger – 2 tsp
- Chopped fresh thyme – 4 tsp
- Crumbled bay leaves – 4
- Soy sauce – ¾ cup

Instructions:
1. Mix the oil, thyme, pepper, bay leaves, garlic, and soy sauce in a bowl.
2. Place chops in a big container or zip-top bag. Cover them with margination. Refrigerate for 24 hours.
3. Preheat grill on high heat and also oil grate. Remove margination from the chops.
4. Cover lamb chops and cook on the grill until brown (takes about 3 minutes). Flip with grilling tongs and continue grilling for five more minutes while covered. The temperature should be 130 F.
5. Remove chops and put them in a dish. Serve hot.

27. Cornish pasties

A part of traditional British food from Cornwall's region, these pasties are everywhere in the Harry Potter series. The recipe of this dish has evolved a great deal since its origin in the 12th century. Triwizard Tournament was a life-changing event for Harry because he saw Lord Voldemort for the first time with his eyes there. Moreover, the death of Cedric Digory made it a

memorable event for Harry Potter fans. Participants of this contest enjoyed Cornish pasties in their lunch when they performed this championship's 3rd task.

Prepare this British dish with our recipe and let your imagination take you to the magical world of the Triwizard Tournament.

Serving size: 6
Cooking time: 1 hour 35 minutes

Ingredients:
- Recipe pastry (for double-crust pie) – 1
- Sliced onion – ½ cup
- Ground black pepper – 1 pinch
- Salt – 1 ½ tsp
- Butter – 2 tbsp
- Sliced potatoes – 2 cups
- Boneless beef steak (thin strips) – ½ lb.

Instructions:
1. Cut pastry into three parts and roll each one to make a rectangle of 8x15 inches. Shape its edges and cut to get the squares of 7-inch. Put them on a baking sheet.

2. On each square of pastry, add a layer of potatoes, add a layer of onion on top, and then beef. Sprinkle some pepper and salt and add butter.
3. Use cold water to moisten the edges of the pastry.
4. Fold edges to give the triangle shape. If you seal tightly, pastries will be juicy because of steam retention.
5. Bake them at about 375 F for an hour.
6. Serve hot along with Ketchup, pickle, or chili sauce.
7. You can also serve cold with sandwiches.

28. Roast chicken

Harry enjoyed roasted chicken in 12 Grimmauld Place. It was the inherited house of the Black family, a noble line of pure-blood wizards. He also had it in the welcoming feast at Hogwarts. You may already know the recipe because it is a typical dish. However, this version has its magical touch, which you cannot deny.

Serving size: 6
Cooking time: 1 hour 40 minutes

Ingredients:
- Whole chicken – 1 lb.
- Margarine – ½ cup
- Celery (without leaves) – 1 stalk
- Pepper and salt – To taste.
- Onion powder – 1 tbsp

Instructions:
1. Preheat the oven to about 350 F.

2. Take a roasting pan and place chicken in it. Season it with pepper and salt from all sides. Also, sprinkle the onion powder.
3. In the cavity of the chicken, put 3 tbsp margarine. Around the exterior of the chicken, arrange dollops of the rest of the margarine. Place celery into a chicken cavity cut into four pieces.
4. In the oven, bake it without any cover for an hour and 15 minutes. The temperature should be around 180 F.
5. Take it off from the heat. Baste it with drippings and melted margarine.
6. Before serving, allow it to rest for at least 30 minutes while covering it in aluminum foil.

29. Casserole

Serving size: 12
Cooking time: 1 hour 45 minutes

Ingredients:
- Melted butter – ¼ cup
- Large eggs – 6
- Shredded Cheddar cheese – 0.75 lb.
- Shredded onion – ½ cup
- Curd cottage cheese – 1 lb.
- Shredded potatoes (pressed) – 3 cups
- Breakfast sausage (sage flavored) – 1 lb.

Instructions:
1. Preheat the oven to about 375 F.
2. Casually grease a square baking dish (9x13 inch).
3. In a big, deep skillet, place the sausage. Cook it on medium heat until it is uniformly brown. Drain, crush and set it aside.

4. In the baking dish, add the butter and shredded potatoes.
5. Line the sides and bottom of the plate with the prepared mixture.
6. Mix the cheddar cheese, eggs, cottage cheese, onion, and sausage in a bowl and pour it on the potato mixture.
7. Bake it in the oven until a knife in the center of it comes out spotless (1 hour).
8. Let it cool for 5-10 minutes. Then, serve.

<u>30. Shepherd's Pie</u>

Servings: 4
Prep Time: 15 minutes
Cook Time: 50 minutes

Ingredients:
- One red onion
- Two small carrots
- One stick celery
- 1 tbsp oil
- 2-3 garlic cloves
- 14 oz diced lamb
- salt and pepper
- 3.4 fl oz red wine
- 15.8 oz tomato passata
- 1 tbsp tomato puree
- One lamb (or beef) stock cube
- 1 tsp mixed herbs
- ½ tsp nutmeg
- ½ tsp cinnamon

- a few dashes of Worcestershire sauce
- Four medium-large white potatoes
- Two medium sweet potatoes
- 1.7-3.5 oz mature cheddar
- 1.7 oz butter
- 1.6 fl oz milk
- salt and pepper
- parsley to garnish

Instructions:
1. Make the lamb ragu base by chopping up the onion, celery, and carrots finely. Add oil into a pan, placing it on medium heat before stirring in vegetables. Keep it moving around for 3-5 minutes until it has started to turn translucent.
2. Peel and crush garlic before adding it to the pan and cooking it for another minute. Take off the vegetables and put them aside in a bowl.
3. Sear the lamb by adding it into the pan, seasoning the meat with salt and pepper, and then turning it after about 20-30 seconds on each side, giving it time to go brown but not cooking it through. Take the lamb off of the pan and set it aside.
4. Deglaze the pan with the red wine and let it steam for 30 seconds as this helps to extract the caramel from the bottom of the pan to improve the taste. The alcohol also burns away, so it is child-friendly.
5. Pour tomato passata and puree into the pan along with the vegetables, lamb, and the assorted seasonings: salt, pepper, mixed herbs, nutmeg, cinnamon, stock cube, and Worchester sauce. Place a lid on the top, turn the heat down to the lowest setting and leave it to simmer for one to two hours. The lamb will also tenderize during this step.

6. In the meantime, you can get the mashed potatoes ready by peeling and washing your potatoes. Leave them in cold water when they have been peeled to keep them from turning brown.

7. Then boil the white and sweet potatoes in separate pots in which there is boiling water, seasoned with salt, for ten to fifteen minutes. Check by testing if easily pierced with a fork.

8. When it's ready, strain off the water using a colander and mash the potatoes in a bowl using a masher, ricer, or fork. Flavor your potatoes with salt, pepper, butter, milk, and cheese, mixing it thoroughly until everything has melted and combined. Then flavor the sweet potatoes with salt, pepper, and butter.

9. To decorate, place the mashed potatoes into a piping bag with a star nozzle.

10. Half an hour before the lamb is ready, take the lid off to encourage the fluid to vaporize and give you a thicker, richer sauce. When prepared, pour it into the bottom of your roasting dish and smooth off with a spatula.

11. Put the mashed potato to the top of the base, beginning with the sweet potato's lightning bolt and then progressing across the outside with the white potato mash.

12. When you're happy with the pattern, bake the shepherd's pie in the oven at 350 degrees F for 25-30 minutes until the potatoes have just started to turn a golden brown.

31. French Onion Soup

Servings: 6
Prep Time: 10 minutes
Cook Time: 1 hour 10 minutes

Ingredients:
- 17.6 oz onions
- 1.7 oz butter
- 1 tbsp olive oil
- Four garlic cloves
- salt and pepper
- Three sprigs rosemary
- Three sprigs thyme
- One bay leaf
- 2.5 fl oz white wine
- 16.9 fl oz strong beef stock
- Six slices of bread
- 1 tbsp butter
- One garlic clove
- 3.5 oz gruyere cheese, grated
- 1 tsp fresh or dried parsley

Instructions:
1. Make the base by peeling and chopping the onions. Remove the skins, slice them in half and then slice them thinly. Use a food processor with a slicing attachment to chop the onions if you aren't used to doing so in large amounts.

2. Place a pan on medium to low heat and then add in your butter and olive oil, swirling it until the butter has melted. Next, add in the onions and allow them to fry for about 10 minutes until they turn soft and translucent. If the onions begin to catch fire, add olive oil to keep them from burning.

3. Peel the cloves of garlic, crush them with a garlic press and then add it to the onions. Season the bass with salt, pepper, finely chopped rosemary, and thyme, and then add to the base. Stir thoroughly and let it continue cooking on low heat for 15-20 minutes.

4. Once the onions are dark and golden, deglaze the pan by pouring in the white wine. Stir through as it bubbles away, then adds in the beef stock and bay leaf and stir it well. Give the soup a taste test, adding in any extra salt and pepper to taste, and then place a lid on top, allowing the soup to simmer for 20 minutes.

5. For the garlic cheese croutons, prepare slices of bread by cutting them small or use baguette slices. Melt the butter in a skillet and smash the garlic before adding. Allow it to fry for a minute.

6. Add the bread and toast for 1-2 minutes on each side until it turns golden.

7. Transfer the soup into ramekins, leaving an inch gap from the top. Place the croutons over the ramekin and sprinkle a generous amount of the cheese over the top. Finish it with some parsley before placing it under the grill for 3-5 minutes until the cheese has melted into the soup. Serve warm.

32. Pumpkin Soup

Servings: 8
Prep Time: 15 minutes
Cook Time: 1 hour

Ingredients:
- One red onion
- Three celery sticks
- Three carrots
- 1 tbsp butter
- One medium pumpkin
- One small butternut squash
- One red pepper
- salt and pepper
- 1 tsp cumin
- 1 tsp paprika
- 1 tsp coriander
- 1 tsp turmeric
- 1 tsp mixed herbs
- One vegetable stock cube
- 8 cups of hot water
- 1 tsp olive oil
- ¼ tsp ground ginger
- 1 tbsp butter
- A sprig of fresh coriander

Instructions:

1. Prepare vegetable base (also known as a mirepoix) by chopping the onion, carrots, and celery into small chunks. Melt butter in the pan and add in the vegetables, stirring it for 3-5 minutes until sweated and glossy. Season it with salt and pepper.
2. Read the rest of the vegetables by peeling the pumpkin and butternut squash and use a serrated knife to cut it into chunks. Keep the seeds to one side for a quick and healthy topping. Remove the seeds from the pepper and chop them into pieces.
3. Add the vegetables into a large pan and stir thoroughly. If the pan seems full, split the content into two. Season the vegetables with mixed herbs, ground coriander, cumin, paprika, and turmeric. Mix well until evenly seasoned, and add in your stock cube with hot water. Cover and leave it to simmer for 30 minutes.
4. While the soup is simmering, prepare your pumpkin seeds as a healthy crouton alternative. Drizzle the oil into a pan, and then add in your pumpkin seeds before seasoning it with salt, pepper, and ginger. Combine it until evenly coated, and then roast it in the oven at 350 degrees F for 15-20 minutes until they turn golden.
5. As soon as the vegetables are soft and cooked through, move them into a bowl and use a hand blender to get a smooth soup. Add more vegetable stock if the soup is too thick.
6. Add in a knob of butter and stir it through until it melted to get a smooth and velvety finish. Season it with any additional salt and pepper and pour it into your bowls. Top it off with a garnish of your roast pumpkin seeds, cream, and coriander just before serving.

33. Mushroom and Lentils Stew

Servings: 4
Prep Time: 10 minutes
Cook Time: 20 minutes

Ingredients:
- 1 tbsp oil
- Two shallots minced
- Two cloves of garlic minced
- 1 ½ cup mushrooms diced
- 1 cup beer (dark beer provides a stronger flavor)
- 1 cup water
- ½ tsp salt
- 2 tsp maple syrup
- 1 tsp thyme
- ¼ tsp ground black pepper
- ½ cup dry green lentils
- One carrot, peeled and cut into thin slices
- One large white potato, peeled and diced
- ⅓ cup green peas
- fresh parsley
- biscuits or bread for serving

Instructions:
1. Using a cast-iron saucepan, heat the oil and add in the shallots and garlic. Sauté for about 5 minutes until the shallots are golden brown.

2. Then add the diced mushrooms and sauté for another 5 minutes, stirring it frequently. Deglaze it with the beer and let it simmer for another 5 minutes.
3. Now add in the water, salt, maple syrup, thyme, black pepper, green lentils, carrot, potato, and green peas.
4. Place a lid over the top and let simmer for about 30 minutes until the lentils and potatoes are tender. Top it with fresh parsley and serve with buttermilk biscuits or bread on the side.

<u>34. Kippers</u>

Yield: 2 servings
Prep time: 5 minutes
Cook time: 20 to 25 minutes

Ingredients:
- One teaspoon salt
- Two teaspoons white vinegar
- Four cold eggs
- Two herring fillets or 1 cup marinated herring in wine sauce
- cream cheese
- Four slices toast
- garlic powder, to serve
- rosemary, to serve
- black pepper, to serve

Instructions:
1. Put 2 inches of water into the saucepan.

2. Add the salt and vinegar to the pan and bring them to a simmer over medium heat.
3. In a separate bowl, crack two cold eggs into two ramekins or custard cups.
4. Use your spatula or spoon's handle to quickly stir the water in one direction, creating a whirlpool action in the water mixture.
5. Pour the two eggs into the center of the whirlpool. The swirling contains the eggs and prevents them from feathering out into the pan.
6. Turn off the heat, cover the pan, and set a timer for 5 minutes. Leave the eggs alone during this time.
7. Use a slotted spoon to remove the eggs and place them on a plate.
8. Repeat with the second batch of 2 eggs.
9. While the second batch of eggs is poaching, place the herring in a preheated cast-iron skillet and cook until both sides are browned. Add a hint of oil throughout if needed to keep the fish from sticking to the pan.
10. Remove and the fish and serve with cream cheese–smeared toast and poached eggs.
11. Sprinkle the garlic powder, rosemary, and black pepper over the eggs.

35. Béchamel

Madam Rosemerta would whip up this deliciousness whenever the students went to Hogsmeade on their weekly visits. The butter and the Parmesan give the dish a wholesome taste that warms you right up after a cold night stroll.

Prep time: 2 to 3 minutes
Cook time: 11 to 13 minutes

Ingredients:

- Two tablespoons butter
- Two tablespoons all-purpose flour
- One ¼ cups milk, heated
- salt
- ground pepper
- ½ cup Parmesan cheese

Instructions:

1. Put the butter in a medium saucepan over medium heat.
2. Once the butter melts, add the flour and stir. The mixture will make a thick paste.
3. Keep stirring the paste until it thins out and begins to bubble. Do not let it brown.
4. Add the hot milk, continuing to stir.
5. Bring the sauce to a boil.
6. Add salt and pepper to taste.
7. Add Parmesan cheese, stirring until it is thoroughly incorporated.
8. Lower the heat and cook for 2 to 3 more minutes while continuously stirring.
9. Remove the sauce from the heat and let it cool for 1 to 2 minutes.

36. Pretzel and Cheese Broomsticks

Active Time: 15 minutes
Yield: 12 broomsticks

Ingredients:

- 12 small pretzel sticks
- Three pieces mozzarella string cheese
- 12 skinny chives

Instructions:
1. Cut each mozzarella stick in thirds, then cut each piece's ends in skinny strips, leaving the cheese connected at the top but fraying the bottom (this is the broom part!).
2. Stick a skinny pretzel stick at the end of each piece of cheese, pushing it into the thick, not frayed side.
3. Wrap a chive around the top of the cheese, right below the pretzel stick. Tie a small knot to look like the top of a broom.
4. Place the broomsticks on a plate and enjoy!

37. Brussels Sprouts

Serves: 6
Preparation Time: 15 minutes
Cooking Time: 45 minutes

Ingredients:
- Brussels sprouts 1 ½ lbs. (ends removed)
- Olive oil 4 tbsp.
- Black pepper ½ tsp.
- Salt 1 tsp.

Instructions:
1. Preheat oven to 400 °F. Place the oven rack in the middle.

2. Place the Brussels sprouts in a bowl. Spread the salt and pepper evenly on top and also mix in the olive oil. (You can also use a zip-lock plastic bag, put in all the ingredients, and shake well to coat evenly.)
3. Layout the Brussels sprouts in a baking pan and place them in the oven.
4. Bake for 30-45 minutes. Stir the pan every few minutes for even browning. When done, the Brussels sprouts should be well browned, crisp on the outside, and soft from inside. Keep adjusting heat to prevent burning.
5. Serve immediately and season with more salt if required.

38. Gillywater

Gillywater is made of Gillyweed (a magical plant) and regular water. When consumed, one develops a temporary set of gills which makes it possible to breath-in oxygen underwater. It also produces webbing between your fingers and toes to aid swimming.

Professor McGonagall and Luna Lovegood both ordered Gillywater at The Three Broomsticks.

Preparation Time: 1 hour
Servings: 15

Ingredients:
- 1-gallon water (filtered or mineral)
- 1 log cucumber, washed and spiralized
- 3 sprigs fresh mint
- ½ lemon juiced
- ice cubes

Instructions:
1. Put the sliced cucumber, mint, and 1/2 juice of the lemon in a wide dish.
2. Refrigerate for one hour.
3. Put into glasses and serve with cucumber to garnish.

39. Harry Potter Pumpkin Howler

Preparation Time: 10 min
Cooking Time: 10 min
Servings: 12

Ingredients:

Filling:
- ¼ tsp. cinnamon
- 1 Tbsp. brown sugar
- 2 Tbsp. pumpkin puree
- 8 oz. mascarpone cheese
- Pinch of salt
- Dash of nutmeg

Howlers Wrap
- 3egg roll wrappers, sliced in quarter pieces
- Red icing
- Black icing Oil for frying
- One beaten egg with
- 1 tsp. water (egg wash)
- 12 eggroll wrappers

Instructions:

1. Mix pumpkin with mascarpone cheese, cinnamon, salt, nutmeg, and brown sugar.
2. Spread the egg roll wrappers with their pointed side upward. Add a Tbsp. of cheese is filling at the center of each.
3. Wet the edges with egg wash and wrap to form small envelopes. Heat oil in a deep pan on medium heat.
4. Cook them in hot oil until golden brown.
5. Make eyes using black icing on each envelope and make lip using red icing.
6. Serve.

40. Fried Tomatoes

Preparation Time: 15 min
Cooking Time: 10 min
Servings: 4

Ingredients:

- Three tablespoons of vegetable oil
- Two tomatoes, ripe and sliced thinly
- All-purpose flour for dredging
- Dash of salt and black pepper
- Toast, for serving

Instructions:

1. Put vegetable oil in a skillet over medium/high heat.
2. Dredge the tomato slices in the all-purpose flour until coated on both sides. Place into the hot oil. Fry for 3 to 5 minutes on each

3. side or until golden.
4. Remove and transfer into a plate lined with paper towels to drain.
5. Powder with black pepper and a pinch of salt.
6. Serve immediately with toast.

41. Bangers & Mash

Preparation time: 10min
Cooking time: 20min
Servings: 4

Ingredients:
- 2 lb. Potatoes
- 8 Cumberland Sausage links, you can use Italian sausage too
- 1 Onion, large
- 1 tbsp. Oil
- 2 tbsp. Flour
- 4 tbsp. Cream
- 4 cups Chicken Stock 2 oz. Butter
- 2 tbsp. Sour Cream 2 tbsp. Mustard
- Black pepper and salt to taste

Instructions:
1. Peel the potatoes, dice them, put them in a pot with water that covers them. Simmer 20 minutes.
2. Prick the sausages with a fork. Brown in a skillet on both sides.
3. Set aside.
4. Add 1 tbsp. oil in the skillet. Slice onion and cook for 5 minutes. Ass 2 tbsp. flour and cook for 1 minute. Add the stock and place the sausages back in the pan. Cook 15 minutes.

5. Drain potatoes and mash them slightly. Add the mustard, sour cream, butter, and cream. Season with black pepper and salt.
6. Serve the sausages over mashed potatoes and enjoy!

42. Corned Beef Sandwich

Preparation Time: 20 min
Cooking Time: 30 min
Servings: 4

Ingredients:
- 8 pcs sliced bread
- 1 lb. corned beef, sliced
- 8 oz. Fontina cheese
- One med onion cut Dijon mustard
- 4 Tbsp. butter

Instructions:
1. To assemble the sandwich, spread Dijon mustard on one side of the bread. Top with corned beef, onion slices, and cheese. Repeat with the other three sandwiches.
2. In a pan grill over low heat, melt butter then, grill the sandwiches, about 3 minutes each side.
3. Cut into triangles before serving.

43. After Quidditch Dinner

Preparation Time: 50 min
Cooking Time: 40 min
Servings: 8

Ingredients:
- 1 lb. ground beef
- One clove garlic, crushed
- ½ cup onion, diced
- ½ cup carrot, diced
- ½ cup frozen peas
- Two medium jalapeno peppers, seeded
- One pack gravy mix prepared according to package directions
- 2 cups mashed potatoes
- ½ cup extra sharp
- Cheddar cheese, shredded
- Smoked paprika
- Cooking spray

Instructions:
1. Preheat the oven to 350 degrees F. Grease a casserole dish with a cooking spray. Set aside.
2. In a large skillet, over medium-high heat, cook ground beef. Stir until it turns brown, about 5 to 7 minutes. Transfer in a bowl. Set aside.
3. Remove much of the oil from the pan. Sauté onion, garlic, carrots, and jalapenos. Stir occasionally until the veggies are softened.
4. Add frozen peas and cook for another 3 minutes.
5. Stir in browned beef and prepared gravy. Mix until combined.

6. Transfer the beef mixture onto the casserole dish. Cover with a layer of mashed potatoes, then top with cheese and a dash of paprika.
7. Bake for 15 minutes. Broil the pie further for 2 minutes until the cheese turns golden brown.
8. Rest for at least 10 minutes before serving.

44. Spiced Dragon Roasted Nuts

Preparation Time: 1 hour
Cooking Time: 1 hour
Servings: 1

Ingredients:
- 1 cup almonds
- ½ tsp salt
- 3 tsp brown sugar
- ½ tsp chili powder
- ½ tsp cayenne powder
- ½ tsp ground cinnamon
- ½ tsp ground cumin
- one egg white

Instructions:
1. Preheat oven to 250 F. Prepares a cooking sheet lined with parchment paper or grease it with some cooking spray. Set aside. In a bowl, mix the spices.
2. Beat the egg white a few times in another bowl. Coat the almonds in it, stirring them with a fork.

3. Put the almonds in the bowl of spices to coat thoroughly. Arrange the almonds in the baking sheet, careful not to overlap the nuts with each other.
4. Bake for 50 minutes or until they turn a nice golden brown.

45. Hagrid's Barbecue Surprise

Preparation Time: 10 min
Cooking Time: 6 min
Servings: 8

Ingredients:
- Two garlic cloves, cut each into four pieces
- One box of frozen meatballs (approximately 3 pounds)
- 2 cups pineapples
- 1 ½ cups maple syrup 2 cups barbecue sauce
- One green pepper, sliced

Instructions:
1. Combine barbeque sauce with maple syrup in a large bowl. Add in the green pepper, pineapple & garlic.
2. Pour ½ of the sauce into the bottom of your Crockpot, and then add in the meatballs.
3. Pour the leftover sauce on top; ensure that everything is evenly covered.
4. Cook on a low-heat setting for 6 hours.

46. Pepper Crusted Roast Beef

Preparation Time: 10 min
Cooking Time: 55 min
Servings: 4-6 plus leftovers

Ingredients:
- One boneless beef roast (approximately 5 ½ to 6 pounds)
- ½ teaspoon ground white pepper
- One tablespoon oil
- ¼ teaspoon ground cayenne pepper
- One teaspoon freshly ground black pepper
- One tablespoon salt

Instructions:
1. Tie the roast with kitchen string and then pat the meat dry using paper towels.
2. Combine pepper with salt & pat the mixture entirely over the meat; cover the meat & set in a refrigerator for a day. Remove the meat from the refrigerator and set it aside at room temperature for 1 to 2 hours before you plan to cook.
3. Preheat your oven to 250 F in advance.
4. Over medium-high heat in a large, heavy skillet, heat the oil until hot. Carefully add the meat and cook for 8 minutes, until it turns brown, 2 minutes per side.
5. Place the meat, fat side up on a wire rack in a shallow roasting pan & roast for 45 minutes per pound until a meat thermometer reflects 140 to 150 F.
6. Cover the meat with foil & set aside for 20 minutes at room temperature.

7. For night 1: Thinly slice 1/3 of the roast diagonally against the grain.

8. For night 2 & 3: Let cool; cover & refrigerate the leftover roast.

47. Fish and Chips

Preparation Time: 20 min
Cooking Time: 20 min
Servings: 4

Ingredients:

For the Fish
- Four white fish fillets such as flounder, cod, halibut, or haddock (each 7 ounces thick)
- 1/3 cup sparkling water
- 2 ounces' all-purpose flour/plain flour
- 1/3 cup dark beer
- 2 ounces corn starch/cornflour
- One teaspoon baking powder
- Pepper & sea salt to taste

For the Chips
- 34 fluids ounces' lard, vegetable oil, or dripping
- 2 pounds peeled potatoes, washed; cut into 1 cm slices and then slice further into 1 cm wide chips

Instructions:

1. Combine two tablespoons of flour with baking powder and corn starch or cornflour in a large bowl; mix well. Lightly season with a pinch of pepper and salt.
2. Whisking well using a fork and then add the water and beer to the flour mixture; continue to mix everything until you get smooth but thick batter-like consistency. Let the batter rest for several minutes inside the fridge.
3. Place the potato chips in a colander & rinse them under cold running tap water.
4. Now, place the potato chips into a pan filled with cold water. Heat the pan over moderate heat and bring it to a gentle boil. Once boiling, decrease the heat & let simmer for a couple of minutes.
5. Carefully drain through a colander and then pat them dry using kitchen paper. Cover them with kitchen paper & keep them inside a fridge until required.
6. In the meantime, arrange the fish fillets on kitchen papers & pat it dry as well. Lightly season with sea salt.
7. Now, over moderate heat in a large, deep saucepan or deep-fat fryer, heat the oil. Work in batches & blanch the chips into the fat for a few minutes. Don't let them turn brown. Once the chips are cooked slightly, immediately remove them from the fat & drain. Keep it to one side.
8. Now, put the two tablespoons of the reserved flour into a large-sized shallow bowl; tossing each fish fillet into the flour; remove any excess flour and then dip the fillets into the batter. Place the coated fillets carefully into the hot oil. Stir-fry until the batter is crisp and golden, for 6 to 8 minutes. Don't forget to turn the fillets occasionally using a large-sized slotted spoon.
9. Once the fillets are cooked through, immediately remove them from the heat source using the same slotted spoon; place them on kitchen

paper to drain and then cover them with the greaseproof paper; try keeping them hot.

10. The next step is to heat the oil over high heat and then carefully cook the chips for a couple of minutes until they turn crisp & golden. Serve immediately with some of the hot fish and your desired condiment.

48. Leek-y Cauldron Soup

Preparation Time: 20 min
Cooking Time: 40 min
Servings: 10

Ingredients:
- One large potato peeled & diced into ½" cubes
- Three large leeks, only white part; thoroughly rinsed & dry, chopped & diced
- 1-pound bacon bits or bacon
- Snipped chives for garnish
- 1 cup butter
- 10 round pretzel rolls, large
- 1 cup flour
- Sharp shredded cheddar for garnish
- 1-quart chicken stock
- Pepper and salt to taste
- 1-quart half and half

Instructions:

1. Add water into a large pot and then add in the potato cubes; bring it to a boil and continue boiling the cubes until tender, over moderate heat. In the meantime, stir-fry the bacon & chop.
2. Scoop the diced bits with approximately ½ cup of water into a large bowl & cook them in the microwave until tender, for a couple of minutes, over high heat.
3. Now, heat the butter over moderate heat in a large soup pot until completely melted. Decrease the heat to low & slowly add in the flour, constantly stirring for a couple of minutes. Slowly add in the chicken stock, continue to mix with a wire whisk. Bring everything together to a boil (stirring frequently) for a couple of more minutes until you start to feel some resistance against the whisk and the liquid thicken.
4. Add in the cream; continue to stir and add in the potatoes, leeks, bacon, pepper, and salt.
5. Let the ingredients heat through, stirring the soup occasionally to prevent it from bubbling. Ensure that you don't bring it to a boil.
6. In the meantime, using a small sharp kitchen knife, cut the center out of your pretzel buns. Cut approximately ¾ of the way through the bun. Spoon the prepared soup into the bowls of your bun & top with fresh chives and shredded cheddar.

49. Hogwarts House Cup Lemon and Garlic Chicken Legs

Preparation Time: 10 min
Cooking Time: 25 min
Servings: 4

Ingredients:
- One lemon, cut in half
- Four chicken leg quarters (with thighs)
- ½ teaspoon paprika
- Four tablespoons melted butter
- ½ teaspoon dried leaf thyme
- One garlic clove, large, minced finely
- ¼ teaspoon of each black pepper & salt

Instructions:
1. Rub all sides of the meat with lemon.
2. Combine garlic with butter, thyme, paprika, pepper, and salt. Spoon or brush the mixture onto the chicken leg quarters, skin side.
3. Arrange the coated meat on the broiler rack. To prevent the fat from burning, put approximately ¼" of water in the bottom of your pan. Broil for 10 minutes about 6" from the heat. Turn & brush the other side with the prepared butter mixture as well. Broil for 8 to 10 more minutes. Brush with the butter mixture again & broil until it turns golden brown and tender.
4. Just before serving, feel free to brush the chicken with more butter mixture, if desired.

50. Hogwarts House Salad

Preparation Time: 25 min
Cooking Time: 0 min
Servings: 4-5

Ingredients:
- 20 yellow cherry tomatoes, sliced in half
- ¼ cup white balsamic vinegar
- Iceberg lettuce; tear & washed
- ½ cup bleu cheese
- One red bell pepper, sliced
- 1/6 cup extra virgin olive oil
- One cucumber, peeled & sliced
- Croutons

Instructions:
1. Toss the tomatoes with cucumbers, peppers, and lettuce in a large-sized salad bowl; toss well.
2. Whisk bleu cheese with the white balsamic vinegar in a small bowl.
3. Whisk olive oil immediately into the bleu cheese- vinegar mixture. Toss with the prepared salad.
4. Add in the croutons. Serve immediately & enjoy.

CHAPTER 2: SWEET RECIPES

51. Licorice Wands

Have you ever wondered what they served back at Ollivanders wand shop? That's right, delicious Licorice Wands. Now you can open your wand shop, thanks to this easy and tasty recipe for licorice wands. Whether you fill your wands with phoenix tail feathers, unicorn hair, or dragon heartstrings—well—that's entirely up to you!

Yield: 24 wands
Prep time: 5 minutes
Cook time: 2 to 3 minutes
Cool time: 1 hour

Ingredients:
- 6 ounces candy melts or almond bark
- 24 licorice twists, any flavor
- candy sprinkles, sugared dots, or other small decorative pieces

Instructions:
1. Put the candy or almond bark in a glass measuring cup and microwave for 30 seconds. Stir.
2. Repeat until the candy is melted and smooth.
3. Dip one end of a licorice twist into the melted candy.
4. Place the candy sprinkles in a separate bowl.
5. Dip the licorice, twist into the candy sprinkles, and roll around, covering the candy coating with as many sprinkles as desired.
6. Repeat steps 3 and 5 with the remaining licorice twists.
7. Cool the twists on a waxed paper sheet for 1 hour or until the coating is firm.

52. Yorkshire Pudding

Yield: 10 to 12 servings
Prep time: 10 minutes
Cook time: 30 to 40 minutes

Ingredients:
- ½ cup beef suet, drippings, butter, or shortening
- ¾ cup all-purpose flour
- ½ teaspoon salt
- Three eggs
- ¾ cup milk

Instructions:
1. Preheat the oven to 450°F.
2. Evenly divide the suet between each of the 12 muffin cups. Set aside.
3. Sift the flour and salt in a small bowl. Set aside.
4. In a medium mixing bowl, combine the eggs and milk and beat until light and foamy.
5. As soon as the oven is at temperature, place the pan with the middle rack's suet. Heat until the fat is smoking hot, which should take 15 to 20 minutes.
6. With a wooden spoon, combine the dry mixture into the egg mixture until just incorporated. Be careful not to overmix.
7. Remove the pan from the oven once the fat is smoking hot and carefully pour it into the pan.
8. Return the pan to the oven and bake for 15 to 20 minutes or until the pudding is puffy and dry.

9. Remove the pan from the oven; now let the pudding cool for some minutes before serving.
10.If there's a little oil remaining on the top of the pudding, drain it carefully before serving.

53. Rice Pudding

Served in the Great Hall, once every month. This pudding even put Draco in a good mood. The foundation of this classic rice pudding is a simple mixture of rice and water or milk, but the toppings are where you can spice things up. Try some colorful berries or fruits in colors that show your House pride, or load up on the chocolate for a more decadent take.

Yield: 6 to 8 servings
Prep time: 15 minutes
Cook time: 10 to 12 minutes

Ingredients:
- 2 cups cooked rice
- ½ cup milk
- ¼ cup cane sugar
- ¼ teaspoon salt
- One tablespoon cocoa powder
- ½ teaspoon vanilla extract
- ⅓ cup semisweet chocolate chips
- whipped cream for garnish
- cinnamon, for garnish

Instructions:
1. Mix all of the ingredients without chocolate chips and garnishes in a medium saucepan over medium-low heat, stirring until thoroughly blended.
2. Turn the heat to low and let simmer.
3. Melt the chocolate chips in the microwave for 30-second intervals until soft and creamy.
4. Add the chocolate chips to the saucepan and stir them in thoroughly with the other ingredients.
5. Stir for 10 to 12 minutes every minute or two to avoid burning.
6. Remove the pan from the heat and let the Rice Pudding stand for 10 minutes before serving. (Or, if preferred, chill for 2 hours and serve.)
7. Garnish with a dollop of whipped cream and lightly sprinkle with cinnamon to serve.

54. Eggnog

Yield: 8 servings
Prep time: 15 minutes
Chill time: 1 hour

Ingredients:
- Four eggs, yolks, and whites separated
- ⅓ cup plus
- One tablespoon cane sugar, divided
- 4 cups milk
- 1 cup heavy whipping cream
- One teaspoon ground cinnamon

- One teaspoon ground nutmeg
- 1 ½ teaspoons vanilla extract

Instructions:
1. Beat the egg yolks at low speed for 2 minutes.
2. Add ⅓ cup of sugar, milk, and cream, and blend until combined thoroughly.
3. Add the spices and blend on low until combined thoroughly.
4. In a separate bowl, beat the egg whites until soft peaks form. Gradually add the remaining one tablespoon sugar to the egg whites while continuously beating and continue beating until stiff peaks form.
5. Add the vanilla extract to the yolk mixture and whisk together until incorporated.
6. Add the egg whites and whisk together until thoroughly blended.
7. Chill for 1 hour and serve

55. Blancmange

Yield: 6 servings
Prep time: 5 minutes
Cook time: 15 minutes
Set time: 6 hours

Ingredients:
- 3 cups milk, divided
- peel of 1 lemon, cut into strips
- Two cinnamon sticks
- ¼ cup cornstarch

- ½ cup cane sugar
- ground cinnamon
- lemon or orange marmalade, to serve

Instructions:
1. Place 1 cup of milk into a saucepan.
2. Add the lemon peel and cinnamon sticks.
3. Turn the heat up to medium and bring the milk to a simmer.
4. Meanwhile, in a small bowl, whisk together the cornstarch and sugar.
5. Whisk the remaining milk into the cornstarch mixture.
6. Once the milk in the pan has begun to simmer, pour the cornstarch mixture into the heated milk in a slow, steady stream.
7. Turn the heat up slightly. Continuously whisk everything together until the mixture comes to a gentle boil.
8. Let boil for 20 seconds, continuously whisking.
9. Remove the pan from the heat.
10. Remove the lemon peel and cinnamon sticks with a slotted spoon.
11. Pour the mixture into a mold or silicone pan, and sprinkle ground cinnamon over the top.
12. Chill for 6 hours to fully set before serving.
13. Serve with the lemon or orange marmalade as a topping.

56. Fresh Fruit Salad

This recipe is for a delicious fruit salad, inspired by the whole fruit, most likely in the care package. A perfect springtime side for any meal, you can customize this recipe to include all of your favorite fruit. All the students loved to dig into these.

Yield: 10 servings
Prep time: 30 minutes

Ingredients:
- half a watermelon
- Two apples
- Two bananas
- One cantaloupe
- 1-pint strawberries
- 1-pint blueberries
- One pineapple
- 1 pound red or green grapes
- whipped cream (optional)

Instructions:
1. Chop all the fruit—minus the blueberries and grapes—into bite-size pieces.
2. Mix the fruit in a large bowl and chill for 2 hours.
3. Serve with dollops of whipped cream, if desired.

57. Knickerbocker Glory

The Knickerbocker Glory is an ice cream extravaganza. With layers of ice cream, fruit, nuts, sauce, and whatever else you'd like, this dessert is perfect for any birthday or special occasion. Try setting up a toppings station so all of your guests can concoct their versions!

Yield: 6 servings
Prep time: 5 to 10 minutes
Cook time: 10 minutes

Ingredients:
- 1.5 quarts vanilla ice cream
- 1 (8-ounce) tub whipped cream
- 4 to 8 ounces frozen mixed berries
- Three tablespoons peanuts, chopped (optional), to garnish
- Raspberry Sauce
- ½ cup cane sugar
- Three tablespoons water
- 12 ounces frozen raspberries

Instructions:
1. To make raspberry sauce: combine the sugar and water in a medium saucepan over medium heat and stir them together until the sugar mostly dissolves.
2. Add the raspberries in small chunks. Wait for each piece to soften slightly before adding the next chunk.
3. Bring the sauce to a gentle boil, continually stirring, remove from the heat and let cool for 2 minutes.

4. If you are using glass serving dishes, place a metal spoon in each serving vessel to dispel heat.
5. Add two tablespoons of raspberry sauce to each glass.
6. Add one small spoonful of vanilla ice cream to each glass.
7. Add one large dollop of whipped cream to each glass.
8. Add a handful of frozen berries to each glass.
9. Repeat with the sauce, ice cream, whipped cream, and berries until each glass is full.
10. Top with the remaining raspberry sauce.
11. Garnish with chopped peanuts, if desired.

58. Chocolate Frogs

Yield: 6
Total time: 2 hours 30 minutes

Ingredients:
- One frog-shaped mold (see the section on Shopping)
- 1¾ ounces (50 g) milk chocolate
- 1¾ ounces (50 g) dark chocolate
- 2⅘ ounces (80 g) marshmallows

Instructions:
1. Break the chocolate into large pieces.
2. Fill a large cauldron with clear water, then place a smaller pot over it, making sure that the water level is always high enough to touch the smaller cauldron's base. Pour the chocolate pieces into the smaller cauldron and gently melt over low heat.

3. When the chocolate forms a smooth ribbon, pour it into the frog molds, dividing it evenly using a Levitation charm, and rotate molds over a sheet of parchment paper (or a plate) so that any excess chocolate runs off leaving just a thin coating.
4. Chill the molds for 30 minutes.
5. Gently melt the marshmallows with a little bit of water to obtain a smooth cream.
6. Take the frogs out of the refrigerator, fill the interior with melted marshmallow, using a knife to smooth everything out, and chill for at least two more hours (the longer your frogs have chilled, the better they will be).
7. Melt the rest of the chocolate again the same way you did earlier and delicately coat the frogs, smoothing away any excess chocolate. Chill for 30 minutes.
8. Carefully remove the frogs from the molds and recite a fidget spell to bring them to life.

59. Pudding Butterscotch Cookies

These chewy cookies are reminiscent of the butterscotch flavor that everyone in Harry Potter loves to enjoy. Make big batches to serve at your party and see how quickly it empties.

Active Time: 8 minutes
Yield: 14 cookies

Ingredients:
- 1 12/ sticks butter, softened
- 1 cup white sugar

- One egg
- One egg yolk
- 1 tsp vanilla extract
- One pinch salt
- 1 tsp baking soda
- 2 cups white, all-purpose flour
- 3.5 ounces packaged butterscotch pudding mix
- 1 cup butterscotch baking chips

Instructions:

1. Mix the butter and the sugar in a large bowl, beating until fluffy.
2. Add the egg, vanilla extract, and the yolk to the whipped butter, mixing slowly and scraping down the bowl to be sure that all the ingredients are fully incorporated.
3. Add the instant pudding mix to the bowl and stir well until the batter is nice and smooth.
4. Place flour, salt, and baking soda into the bowl and stir together until smooth.
5. Fold in the butterscotch chips.
6. Scoop the cookie dough onto a parchment-lined sheet tray, making dough balls that are about 2 tbsp in size.
7. Bake the cookies in a preheated 350 degrees F oven for about 10 min.
8. Cool the cookies for 5-6 minutes before moving them to a cooling rack. Enjoy!

60. Butterbeer Ice Cream

Active Time: 30 minutes
Yield: 4 servings

Ingredients:
- 2 ½ cups heavy cream, cold
- One can of sweetened condensed milk, cold
- ¼ cup butter
- ½ cup dark brown sugar
- 1 tsp vanilla extract

Instructions:
1. Place ¼ cup heavy cream, butter, dark brown sugar, and vanilla in a saucepan. Heat over medium-high and let the mix come to a full boil. Cook, constantly stirring, for about 5-10 minutes or until a thick caramel sauce has formed. Remove from the heat and let the mix cool.
2. In a mixer fitted with a whisk attachment, whip the two ¼ cups of heavy cream until stiff peaks form. Add the cold sweetened condensed milk to the whipped cream and whip again until light and fluffy.
3. Fold in the chilled caramel sauce to the whipped cream mix.
4. Pour the mixture into a safe container for the freezer, cover, and place in the freezer for about 5 hours to firm completely.
5. Scoop and serve!

61. Lemon Candy

Dumbledore loves lemon sherbet so much that he even made it his secret password! You will enjoy these lemon jelly candies just as much. Maybe you will make your secret passwords "Lemon Jelly"! Madam Rosmerta would always whip up some out of thin air whenever Dumbledore would visit.

Active Time: 15 minutes
Yield: about 20 servings

Ingredients:
- 2 tbsp plain gelatin
- One ¼ cup water
- 2 cups white granulated sugar
- 6 ounces lemon-flavored jello packets (powdered)
- ½ cup fresh lemon juice
- 1 tsp fresh grated lemon zest

Instructions:
1. Prepare an eight-inch square cake pan by lining it with foil and spraying the foil with cooking spray. Set aside for now.
2. Place 1/3 cup of the water in a small bowl and sprinkle with the plain gelatin. Let sit until the gelatin becomes firm.
3. In a small pot, add the sugar and remaining water and bring to a boil. Cook the sugar to the hardball stage or until it reaches 260 degrees on a candy thermometer.
4. Remove the sugar from the heat and stir in the lemon powdered gelatin and the firm, plain gelatin.

5. Add the lemon juice and zest, and stir the mix until smooth.
6. Pour the hot mixture into the prepared cake pan, then cover and refrigerate.
7. Once chilled and firm, cut the candies into your desired shape. Toss in extra white sugar, and then enjoy!

62. Bertie's Bean Bark

Bertie Bott's store is known to have every flavor of jelly bean imaginable- even some unimaginable flavors! Make this delicious and easy-to-make dessert to celebrate tasty jelly beans, just like at the Harry Potter store.

Active Time: 15 minutes
Yield: 10 servings

Ingredients:
- 1 ½ pound white chocolate chips
- 1 tbsp coconut oil
- 2 cups jelly beans

Instructions:
1. Line a rimmed sheet tray with parchment and set it aside.
2. Melt the chocolate in a double boiler, frequently stirring so that the chocolate does not burn.
3. Stir the butter into the melted chocolate until it is melted.
4. Pour the chocolate onto the prepared sheet tray and use an offset spatula to spread it evenly.
5. Sprinkle the jelly beans over the chocolate, distributing them evenly.

6. Let the chocolate harden at room temperature or place it in the fridge to speed up the process.
7. Break the bark into pieces and enjoy!

63. Honeyduke's Pops

You should beware of eating a lollipop from Honeyduke's as they may burn your tongue! However, this recipe is perfectly safe and delicious, making Harry Potter lovers an excellent treat everywhere. The recipe captures the essence of the classic lollipop minus the burn.

Active Time: 10 minutes
Yield: 12 servings

Ingredients:
- 1 cup light corn syrup
- 2/3 cup white granulated sugar
- ½ tbsp lemon candy flavoring
- 4 drops yellow food coloring

Instructions:
1. Prepare your lollipop mold by placing the lollipop sticks in the mold in advance then set aside.
2. Add the corn syrup and sugar into a small saucepan and bring to a boil. Cook until the mixture on a candy thermometer reaches 300 degrees F.
3. Remove the pot from the heat and quickly stir in the food coloring and flavoring.
4. Pour the hot sugar into the lollipop mold, making sure to cover the end of the stick entirely in the candy, so it sticks well.

5. Let the lollipops harden and cool before popping out of the mold and enjoying!

64. Cockroach Chocolates

Active Time: 8 minutes
Yield: 10 servings

Ingredients:
- 1 pound soft caramel candies
- 3 tbsp water
- 1 ½ cup chopped, toasted pecans
- 1 cup puffed rice cereal
- 3 cups dark chocolate chips
- 1 ½ tbsp coconut oil

Instructions:
1. Start preparing a baking sheet with parchment and spray with cooking spray. Set aside
2. Place the caramels and water in a large saucepan and heat over medium heat, frequently stirring until melted.
3. Mix the pecans and rice cereal into the caramel mix and then scoop the mixture with a tablespoon, dropping it onto the prepared sheet tray in small dollops.
4. Let the caramels cool until firm.
5. Then, melt the dark chocolate chips and coconut oil, stirring until smooth.

6. Dip the caramels into the chocolate, coating them completely, and then placing them back on the sheet tray until firm.
7. Enjoy!

65. English Toffee

Mrs. Weasley makes toffee each year, and it was the first package that Harry got at Christmas from the Weasleys. This recipe gives you something to look forward to and to sure any homesickness you may be experiencing like Harry was that first year.

Active Time: 15 minutes
Yield: 10 servings

Ingredients:
- ½ pound unsalted butter
- 1 cup white granulated sugar
- ¼ cup water
- ½ tsp sea salt
- ½ cup chocolate chips
- 1 cup chopped, toasted pecans

Instructions:
1. Begin by getting out a 9x13 flat sheet pan and setting it aside.
2. Place the butter, sugar, water, and sea salt in a pot and boil over medium-high heat.
3. Cook until it reaches 300F, stirring occasionally.
4. Pour the hot toffee onto the flat sheet tray.

5. Let the toffee cool at room temperature until very firm.
6. Melt the chocolate chips and then spread the melted chocolate over the top of the toffee.
7. Sprinkle the toffee evenly with the chopped nuts, and then let the chocolate firm.
8. Break into pieces and enjoy!

66. Rock Cakes

Active Time: 8 minutes
Yield: 10 servings

Ingredients:
- 1 cup all-purpose white flour
- 8 tbsp butter, cut into pieces, cold
- 1 tsp baking powder
- ¼ cup white granulated sugar
- ½ cup dried cranberries
- ½ cup mini chocolate chips
- ¼ cup chopped, sliced almonds (toasted)
- One egg, room temperature
- 2 tbsp whole milk

Instructions:
1. Mix the all-purpose flour and baking powder in a big bowl.
2. Add the cold butter and cut it in until the mix resembles fine crumbles.
3. Add the sugar, cranberries, chocolate chips, and sliced almonds to the mix and stir well.

4. Add the egg and milk and stir, using your hands if needed, until a nice stiff dough has formed.
5. Place dough balls, about 1- 1 ½ inches in size, on a parchment-lined sheet tray and then bake in a 350 degree F oven.
6. Bake for about 10-12 minutes until the bottoms begin to brown.
7. Cool on a cooling rack, and then enjoy!

67. Golden Snitch Truffles

Active Time: 45 minutes
Yield: 20 truffles

Ingredients:
- 8 ounces dark chocolate, chopped
- 2/3 cup heavy whipping cream
- 1 tbsp salted butter, soft
- ½ tsp vanilla extract
- ½ cup gold sprinkles

Instructions:
1. Place the chopped chocolate together with the butter in a large metal bowl.
2. Heat the heavy whipping cream in a small pot over medium heat. Bring to a boil, then remove from heat immediately and stir in the vanilla extract.
3. Pour over the chocolate the hot cream and allow it to sit for about 2 minutes.
4. Whisk the chocolate and cream until homogenous.

5. Scoop the chocolate into tablespoon-sized balls and place on a parchment-lined sheet tray.
6. Let the chocolates firm at room temperature or in the fridge.
7. Once hard, roll the truffles, use your hands into smooth balls, and roll in the gold sprinkles to coat.
8. Serve or store in the fridge!

68. Peppermint Toads

The peppermint toads in Harry Potter-like to hop around inside your stomach after you eat them. These are for those who don't like chocolate too much and spice their lives with a little peppermint.

Active Time: 15 minutes
Yield: 10 toads

Ingredients:
- 2 cups white candy chocolate
- 5 drops peppermint candy flavoring
- 5 drops red gel food coloring

Instructions:
1. Place a frog or toad-shaped chocolate candy mold on a flat sheet tray.
2. Now you have to melt the white chocolate over a double boiler, stirring continually.
3. Once melted, add the peppermint flavoring and the red food coloring to the chocolate, stirring well.

4. Pour the chocolate into the molds, then let harden at room temperature for about an hour.
5. Pop the chocolates out of the mold and enjoy!

69. Dragon Roasted Nuts

You may remember another of the Weasley brother's inventions where a small dragon would breathe fire on chestnuts to roast them. While you do not need a dragon to make this recipe, it is surely just as tasty! They can be your crunchy go-to treats for all time every day!

Active Time: 15 minutes
Yield: 6 servings

Ingredients:
- 2 pounds chestnuts in the shells
- 1 tbsp fresh chopped rosemary
- 8 tbsp melted butter
- 1 tsp sea salt
- 1/8 tsp ground nutmeg

Instructions:
1. Spread the chestnuts on a large piece of aluminum foil and then carefully cut an x in the top of each nut with a sharp knife. Place the nuts in a large bowl of hot water to soak for one minute.
2. Drain the nuts and then toss in a bowl with the remaining ingredients.
3. Spread the chestnuts back on the foil and then pull the foil's edges upward, making a little bowl. You do not want to wrap the nuts

completely in foil but leave a small opening in the foil's top for steam to escape.
4. Bake the chestnuts in a preheated 425 degrees F oven for 40 minutes. The edges of the scored x's will start to peel back when the nuts are done.
5. Remove from the foil and serve with more salt if needed.

70. Banana Fritters

Servings: 6
Preparation Time: 10 minutes
Cooking Time: 5 minutes

Ingredients:
- Milk ½ cup
- Bananas 3 (mashed)
- All-purpose flour 2 cups
- Salt ½ tsp.
- Baking Powder 3 tsp.
- Eggs 2 (whisked)
- Margarine or Butter 1 tbsp. (melted)
- Cinnamon powder ¼ tsp.
- Icing sugar/powdered sugar 2 tbsp. (for serving)
- Vegetable oil as needed for deep frying

Instructions:

1. Combine the milk and bananas in a medium-sized bowl. Add in the flour, baking powder, salt, cinnamon powder, eggs, and margarine. Mix well until you get a smooth batter.
2. Heat oil in a deep frying pan to 365 °F.
3. Place spoon-sized batter balls carefully into the preheated oil. Fry them until they are brown from both sides, turning over when needed. Once done, take them out on paper towels to drain the excess oil.
4. Sprinkle powdered sugar over the fritters and serve them warm.

71. Dumbledore's Pensieve

Serving Size: 4
Prep time: 10 minutes
Total Prep time: 5 minutes

Ingredients:
- One jelly packet, blue-colored
- ¼ cup hot water
- 5-6 Ice cubes

Instructions:
1. Make jelly using 2/3 packs of the jelly package as per instructions on the box.
2. Allow the jelly to cool and set.
3. Mix the remaining jelly with hot water, then add some ice cubes.

72. Madam Poppy Pomfrey's chocolate shake

Preparation Time: 20 minutes
Cooking time: 5 minutes
Servings: 1

Ingredients:
- Milk – 1 cup
- Chocolate syrup – 1tbsp
- Chocolate ice cream – 2 cups

Instructions:
1. Soften ice cream by keeping it outside the freezer for a few moments.
2. Place it with milk in a blender (add more milk to get thin consistency).
3. Put chocolate syrup in.
4. Keep blending until smooth.
5. Pour into the glass. Enjoy!

73. Cream Puffs

Preparation Time: 15 minutes
Cooking Time: 20 Minutes
Servings: 6

Ingredients:
- 1 box cake mix (lemon / orange)
- One egg yolk
- One package (500g/18oz) cream cheese
- 2 Tbsp. water
- ¼ cup sugar
- ¼ cup walnuts (optional)

Instructions:
1. Preheat the oven to 375 degrees F.
2. Mix the egg yolk, cream cheese, water, and cake mix by hand until the dough is formed.
3. Mix sugar and nuts in a small bowl.
4. Form the dough into golf ball-sized balls.
5. Roll balls in the sugar and nuts until fully covered.
6. Put them on a greased baking tray and bake for 10-12 minutes.
7. The pastries should look puffed and be golden underneath.
8. Serve with cream or custard if desired.
9. You can leave out the nuts and only use sugar if you prefer.
10. Use a variety of cake mixes if you want to try different flavors.

74. Chocolate Peanut Clusters

Preparation Time: 15 minutes
Cooking Time: 2 minutes
Servings: 18

Ingredients:
- 1 (12-ounce) package peanut butter chips
- 1 (12-ounce) package semi-sweet chocolate chips
- 12 ounces raw Spanish peanuts

Instructions:
1. In a bowl, place the peanut butter chips and chocolate chips and microwave on High for about 1½-2 minutes or until melted, stirring after every 20 seconds.
2. Remove from microwave and stir until smooth.
3. Add the peanuts and stir to combine.

4. Spoon the desired sized mixture onto waxed paper and set aside to cool completely before serving.
5. Serving Suggestions: Enjoy these clusters with the rich, fruity sweetness of a late-bottled vintage port.

Variation Tip: You can also use roasted peanuts instead of Spanish peanuts.

75. Butterbeer Popcorn

Preparation Time: 15 minutes
Cooking Time: 10 minutes
Servings: 12

Ingredients:
- 12 cups air-popped popcorn
- One teaspoon baking soda
- ¼ teaspoon ground nutmeg
- Four teaspoons pure vanilla extract
- One teaspoon almond extract
- One teaspoon butter extract
- ¾ teaspoon rum extract
- 1 cup sugar
- Eight tablespoons unsalted butter
- Three tablespoons blackstrap molasses
- One tablespoon water
- ½ teaspoon coarse kosher salt

Instructions:

1. Line and set aside a large baking sheet with parchment paper. In a large bowl, place the popcorn, and set it aside.
2. In a small bowl, sift together the baking soda and nutmeg.
3. In another bowl, add all the extracts and mix well.
4. In a medium, heavy-bottomed saucepan, add the sugar, butter, molasses, water, and salt over medium heat and cook until a candy thermometer reads to 305 degrees F, stirring occasionally.
5. Now remove and stir in the baking soda mixture and extract mixture.
6. Place the mixture over the popcorn and toss to coat well.
7. Place the popcorn onto the prepared baking sheet and, with a spatula, spread in an even layer.
8. Set aside to cool completely.
9. Break it apart and serve.

Serving Suggestions: Serve with a drizzling of melted chocolate.

Variation Tip: If Butterbeer popcorn is too sticky, then dry it in the oven. Place the popcorn onto a baking sheet and bake it in a 200 degrees F oven for 20-30 minutes, tossing after every 10 minutes.

76. Lemon Drop Bark

Preparation Time: 15 minutes
Cooking Time: 2 minutes
Servings: 12

Ingredients:
- 1 (12-ounce) package white chocolate chips
- ¾ cup lemon drop candies

Instructions:
1. In a bowl, put the white chocolate chips and microwave on High for about 1½-2 minutes or until melted, stirring after every 20 seconds.
2. Remove from microwave and stir until smooth.
3. In a resealable plastic bag, place lemon drop candies.
4. Place this bag into another resealable bag and seal bot bags.
5. With a rolling pin, crack candies into small pieces.
6. Add the candy pieces into melted white chocolate and stir to combine.
7. Place the mixture onto a piece of foil and spread to about ¼-inch thickness.
8. Refrigerate for at least 30 minutes or until set.
9. Break bark into small pieces and serve.

Serving Suggestions: Serve with the garnishing of candied lemon peel.

77. Unicorn Hot Chocolate

Preparation Time: 10 minutes
Cooking Time: 5 minutes
Servings: 4

Ingredients:
- 2 cups milk
- 2 cups half-and-half
- 1 cup white chocolate chips
- One teaspoon vanilla extract
- Pink food coloring, as required
- Four tablespoons whipped cream
- Two tablespoons sprinkle

Instructions:
1. In a medium saucepan, place the milk, half-and-half, white chocolate chips, and vanilla extract over medium heat and cook until heated through, beating continuously.
2. Remove from the heat and stir in the food coloring.
3. Transfer the hot chocolate into mugs and top with whipped cream.
4. Garnish with sprinkles and serve.

Serving Suggestions: You can enjoy this hot chocolate with the drizzling of caramel sauce.

78. Magic Wands

Preparation Time: 15 minutes
Cooking time: 0 minutes
Servings: 30

Ingredients:
- 1 (16-ounce) container prepared vanilla frosting
- ½ cup sprinkles
- 1 (15-ounce) package pretzel rods

Instructions:
1. In 2 separate bowls, place the frosting and sprinkles, respectively.
2. Dip each pretzel rod into the frosting and then coat it with sprinkles.
3. Arrange the sticks onto a parchment paper-lined baking sheet and set them aside until set.
4. Serving Suggestions: you can serve these magic wands with a drizzling of melted chocolate.

79. Yorkshire Pudding

Preparation Time: 10 minutes
Cooking time: 20-25 minutes
Servings: 6 puddings

Ingredients:
- Four eggs (200 ml)
- 1 cup milk (250ml)
- 1 cup flour (250ml)
- Pinch of salt
- ¼ cup rendered fat or vegetable oil

Instructions:
1. Preheat your oven to 430°F
2. Preheat your oven to a 430°F Muffin tray. Place in the oven for 5 or 6 minutes.
3. Meanwhile, in a large bowl, mix the salt and the flour. Create a depression in the center add in the eggs and a bit of milk. Whisk until smooth, and then carefully add in the remaining milk.
4. Carefully and slowly, remove the tray from the oven and pour in the pudding batter equally into the tins (watch out for the piping hot oil). Quickly return the tray to the oven and bake for 23-25 minutes, or until the puddings are golden-brown and have risen well.
5. Serve.

80. Mrs.Weasley's Fudge

Preparation Time: 10 minutes
Cooking time: 20 minutes
Servings: 20 pieces

Ingredients:
- 3 cups white sugar
- 2/3 cup Dutch-processed cocoa
- 1/8 tsp salt
- 1 1/2 cups milk
- 1/4 cup butter
- 1 tsp vanilla extract

Instructions:
1. Line an 8 x 8-inch pan with baking paper and grease slightly using a cooking spray.

2. In a medium saucepan, combine sugar, salt, and cocoa and stir together using a wooden spoon. Add the milk and stir again.
3. Stir over medium heat, stirring continuously until the mixture starts to boil, approx. 15 minutes. Reduce heat and stop stirring. When the temperature reaches 235°F, approx. Thirty minutes, remove the pot and add in the butter and vanilla, making sure not to stir the mixture. Now the mixture must reach room temperature.
4. Stir the mixture with a wooden spoon or until it starts to lose some of its gloss (approx. 6-8 minutes).
5. Quickly spread the mixture in the cake pan and let cool completely, preferably overnight.
6. Cut into pieces and serve.

81. Black Pudding

Prep Time: 10 min
Cooking Time: 1 hour
Servings: 10

Ingredients:
- 2 ½ tsp salt
- 1 ½ cups steel-cut oatmeal
- 1 ½ tsp pepper
- 1 tsp allspice (ground)
- 1 cup milk
- One onion (yellow, large, chopped)
- 2 cups pork fat (finely diced)
- 4 cups pigs blood (fresh)

Instructions:

1. Preheat the oven to 325 F.
2. Grease 2 glass loaf pans (or parchment-lined metal loaf pan). Stir one teaspoon of salt into the fresh blood.
3. Boil 2 ½ cups of water and add the oats.
4. Cook oats until tender, not overly soft (around 15 minutes). Sieve the blood to remove any lumps, then stir in the remaining salt, pepper, allspice, onion, milk, and fat.
5. Pour evenly into the two pans, cover with tin foil and bake for 1 hour or until firm.
6. Allow them to cool completely.
7. Wrap in cling-wrap and freeze for long-term use or store in the refrigerator for up to 1 week.
8. To serve, slice off a piece around the same thickness as a slice of bread. Fry in a pan until the edges are browned and slightly crisp. Eat with breakfast or even in a salad.

82. Pumpkin Juice

Preparation Time: 10 minutes
Servings: 2 servings

Ingredients:

- 8 ounces apple cider
- 3 Tbsp. pumpkin puree
- 1/8 tsp pumpkin pie spice
- 1/8 tsp cinnamon
- 1/8 tsp nutmeg

Instructions:

1. In a saucepan, stir the pumpkin purees and spices and heat until warm. Slowly stir in the apple cider until well combined. Heat and stir until warm.
2. Remove from heat and serve.
3. Alternately, to serve the pumpkin juice cold, place all the ingredients in a blender along with some ice and blend until smooth.

83. Honeyduke'ss Coconut Ice

Preparation Time: 2 hrs. 10 minutes
Cooking time: 0 minutes
Servings: 25 bars

Ingredients:
- Cooking spray
- 2 cups sifted powdered sugar
- 1/4 tsp cream of tartar
- 1 14 oz can condensed milk
- 1/2 tsp vanilla extract
- 3 1/2 cups unsweetened shredded coconut
- 2-3 drops pink food coloring

Instructions:

1. Cover an 8-inch square cake pan with baking paper.
2. In a large bowl, combine sugar and cream of tartar. Add in condensed milk and vanilla extract and mix until well combined. Add shredded coconut and mix again.
3. Divide the mixture in half. Color one-half of the mix with the pink food coloring and knead until evenly colored.

4. Press pink mixture into the pan and smooth the surface with the back of the spoon. Top with the remaining mixture and press down until smooth.
5. Refrigerate for 3 hours or until firm. Cut into pieces and serve.

84. Exploding Bonbons

Preparation Time: 20 minutes
Cooking Time: 1½ minutes
Servings: 15

Ingredients:
- 1 (7-ounce) jar marshmallow crème
- 2 2/3 cups sweetened shredded coconut, toasted
- One teaspoon vanilla extract
- Pinch of salt
- 1 (5-ounce) milk chocolate candy bar, chopped
- 1½ teaspoons shortening

Instructions:
1. In a large bowl, place and mix well.
2. Cover the bowl and refrigerate for at least 1 hour.
3. Make about 1-inch balls from the mixture.
4. Arrange the balls onto a waxed paper-lined baking sheet and refrigerate for about 3 hours or until firm.
5. In a microwave-safe bowl, place chocolate candy bar and shortening and microwave on high for about 1-1½ minutes, stirring after every 20 minutes.
6. Remove from microwave and stir until smooth.

7. Dip balls into shortening mixture evenly and again arrange onto a waxed paper-lined baking sheet.
8. Refrigerate for 2 hours before serving.

85. Butterbeer Muddy Buddies

Preparation Time: 20 minutes
Cooking Time: 1 minute
Servings: 12

Ingredients:
- 12 ounces butterscotch chips
- ½ cups salted butter, melted
- One teaspoon imitation butter extract
- One teaspoon vanilla extract
- 8 cups rice Chex cereal
- ¼ cup toffee bits
- 1½ cups powdered sugar

Instructions:
1. In a microwave-safe bowl, place the butterscotch chips and microwave on 50% power for about 1 minute, stirring after every 20 seconds.
2. Remove from the microwave and stir until smooth.
3. Add the melted butter, butter extract, and vanilla extract and beat until well combined.
4. In a large paper bag, place the cereal, toffee bits, and butter mixture and shake to coat well.
5. Put the mixture into a baking sheet and spread it in an even layer.
6. Set aside for about 20 minutes.

7. In another large paper bag, place the mixture and powdered sugar and
    shake to coat.

86. Chocolate Spiders

Preparation Time: 15 minutes
Cooking Time: 2 minutes
Servings: 20

Ingredients:
- 1 pound chocolate confectioners' coating, chopped
- 1 (8½-ounce) package chow mein noodles

Instructions:
1. In a microwave-safe bowl, place the chocolate coating and microwave
    on High for about 1½-2 minutes or until melted, stirring after every 20
    seconds.
2. Remove from microwave and stir until smooth.
3. Add the chow mein noodles and stir to combine.
4. Spoon the desired sized mixture onto waxed paper and set aside to cool
    completely before serving.

87. Wingless Snatchers

Preparation Time: 20 minutes
Cooking Time: 3 minutes
Servings: 15

Ingredients:
- 3½ cups white baking chips, divided
- 3 ounces cream cheese, softened
- ½ cup butter softened
- Two tablespoons dark rum
- ¼ teaspoon vanilla extract
- Two tablespoons shortening

Instructions:
1. In a microwave-safe bowl, place 1½ cups of baking chips and microwave on high for about 1-1½ minutes, stirring after every 20 minutes.
2. Remove from microwave and stir until smooth.
3. In a small bowl, place cream cheese and butter and beat until smooth.
4. Add rum and vanilla and mix well.
5. Add melted chips and beat until well combined.
6. Cover the bowl and refrigerate for about 1 hour or until set.
7. Make about 1-inch balls from the mixture.
8. Arrange the balls onto a waxed paper-lined baking sheet and refrigerate for about 2 hours or until firm.
9. In a microwave-safe bowl, place remaining baking chips and shortening and microwave on high for about 1-1½ minutes, stirring after every 20 minutes.
10. Remove from microwave and stir until smooth.

11. Dip balls into shortening mixture evenly and again arrange onto a waxed paper-lined baking sheet.
12. Refrigerate for about 2 hours before serving.

88. Chocolate Gateau

Preparation Time: 15 minutes
Cooking Time: 52 minutes
Servings: 8

Ingredients:
- 4½ ounces bittersweet chocolate, chopped
- ½ cup butter, chopped
- ½ cup sugar, divided
- Three eggs, separated
- One teaspoon vanilla extract
- ½ teaspoon salt

Instructions:
1. Preheat the oven to 350 degrees F.
2. Grease a 6×3-inch springform pan.
3. In a microwave-safe bowl, place chocolate and butter and microwave on High for about 1½-2 minutes or until melted, stirring after every 20 seconds.
4. Remove from microwave and stir until smooth.
5. Set aside to cool slightly.
6. In the bowl of a stand mixer. Place ¼ cup of sugar and egg whites and beat on high speed until stiff peaks form.
7. Meanwhile, in another bowl, place the remaining sugar and egg yolks and beat until pale yellow and doubled in size.

8. I the bowl of the cooled chocolate mixture, add the vanilla extract and salt and beat until well combined.
9. Add the chocolate mixture into the bowl of egg yolks and beat until well combined.
10. Add the egg whites mixture and gently stir to combine.
11. Place the mixture into the prepared pan evenly.
12. Bake for about 45-50 minutes or until a toothpick inserted in the center comes out clean.
13. Remove to place onto a wire rack to cool for at least 10 minutes.
14. Carefully invert the cakes onto the platter and serve warm.

90. Pumpkintini

Preparation Time: 10 minutes
Servings: 2

Ingredients:
- Ice, as required
- Six tablespoons white rum
- Six tablespoons pumpkin puree
- Two tablespoons coconut milk
- 1½ tablespoons pure maple syrup
- ½ tablespoon whiskey
- Pinch of ground cinnamon
- Pinch of ground cloves
- Pinch of ground ginger
- Two graham cracker sheets, crushed finely

Instructions:
1. Fill the cocktail shaker with ice cubes within 1-inch of the top.
2. Add the remaining ingredients except for graham cracker into the cocktail shaker.
3. Cover the cocktail shaker with a lid and shake to combine thoroughly.
4. Wet the edge of each glass and dip the rim into graham cracker crumbs.
5. Strain drink and pour into prepared glasses.
6. Serve immediately.

Serving Suggestions: Serve with the sprinkling of cinnamon.
Variation Tip: you can substitute the pumpkin puree with pumpkin pie filling.

91. Christmas Cake

Prep Time: 30 min
Cooking Time: 3 hours
Servings: 10

Ingredients:
- 1 kg mixed dried fruit of your choice
- 150 ml sherry, rum, brandy, or brewed tea (plus a little extra for feeding)
- Two lemons or oranges (zest and juice)
- 250g unsalted butter (softened)
- 250g brown sugar
- 200g plain flour
- Four eggs
- 2 tsp mixed spice

- 2 tsp vanilla extract
- 100g almonds (or other nuts)

Instructions:
1. Place fruit and alcohol/tea in a bowl, along with the lemon juice and lemon zest. Let the mixture stand overnight.
2. Heat oven to 160 °C (320 °F).
3. Butter and line a cake tin with enough baking paper to stick out above the tin by around 2.5cm and wrap the entire tin with paper secured with string or staples.
4. Beat the butter, vanilla, and sugar until creamy.
5. Add the flour, spice, soaked fruit plus liquid, and nuts.
6. Mix the butter and fruit mix and scrape it all into the cake tin.
7. Make a dent in the middle of the cake with a spoon. Bake for 1 ½ hour.
8. Reduce heat to 140 °C (285 °F) and cover the cake with tin foil. Bake for 45 minutes to 1 hour or until the knife comes out clean when poked in the middle of the cake.
9. Cool in the tin.
10. Pull the cake out of the jar and cover it with grease-proof parchment. Keep in a sealed container for six months, opening every two weeks to poke and add a little of the alcohol or tea you choose.

92. Mince Pies

Prep Time: 5 minutes
Cooking Time: 15 minutes
Serving: 16

Ingredients:
- 500ml all-purpose flour
- 250ml margarine (for baking)
- 50ml ice water
- 3ml salt
- 15ml vinegar
- One egg yolk (keep white for brushing)
- 500g minced fruit
- 1 tsp caster sugar (for dusting)

Instructions:
1. Mix the flour, salt, and margarine in a food processor.
2. Beat the vinegar, egg yolk, and water together. Then add the mixture to the dry ingredients.
3. Once you have a firm dough, wrap in cling-wrap and refrigerate for 1 hour.
4. Preheat oven to 220 °C (430 °F).
5. Roll the dough out thinly, then cut into rounds about 10 cm in diameter.
6. Fit rounds into a greased muffin pan. Fill each round with minced fruit.
7. Dampen the edges of the pastry, then add a 7 cm round on top.
8. Squeeze edges together gently to seal.

9. Prick the top of the pies with a toothpick to allow steam to escape. Brush lightly with the egg whites and place them in the oven for 10 to 15 minutes.
10. Remove once golden brown and sprinkle with caster sugar while still hot.
11. Allow to cool and serve as part of your lunch or dinner feast.

93. Charmed Cherry Soda

Prep Time: 5 minutes
Cooking Time: 10 minutes
Servings: 2

Ingredients:
- 2 cups black cherries
- 1/2 cup sugar
- 1/2 water
- One tablespoon lemon juice
- Setzer Soda Water
- One-shot plain vodka
- One-shot lemon-flavored vodka Ice

Instructions:
1. Add cherries, sugar, lemon juice, and water to a saucepan and cook for 10 minutes on a simmer with occasional stirring.
2. Mash the raspberries as you cook the cherries. Strain the cherry mixture and pour it into a jar. Refrigerate for at least 1 hour, then serve.

94. Sorting Hat Cupcakes

Another way to add a vintage sorting hat to the dinner table is the sorting hat cupcake. These are ordinary cupcakes with a magical twist of Harry Potter. So, spread this magic in your kitchen and make these cupcakes with chocolate hats and cookies.

Serving Size: 12
Prep time: 10 minutes
Total Prep time: 25 minutes

Ingredients:

For Hats
- 12 chocolate kisses
- 6 Oreos, cream removed
- ¼ cup chocolate chips, melted

For buttercream
- ¼ cup heavy cream
- 1 ½ cups butter, softened
- 6 cups powdered sugar
- 2 Tbsp. Butterscotch syrup
- Pinch kosher salt
- Red, yellow, green, and blue food coloring
- Gold sprinkles, for garnish
- One box white cake mix,

Instructions:

1. Set the oven to 350 degrees F.
2. Line a muffin tray with paper liners.
3. Prepare batter using the cake mix as per the instructions on the box.
4. Divide the batter into the liner and bake for 25 minutes.
5. Allow the cupcakes to cool.
6. Meanwhile, make small hats using chocolate shreds at the center of the Oreo cookie.
7. Allow them to sit for 15 minutes.
8. Blend butter with sugar, cream, butterscotch, and salt until creamy.
9. Reserve 1/3 of the frosting and divide the remaining frosting into four separate bowls.
10. Add red, blue, green, and yellow food color to each of the four bowls.
11. Mix well and fill the center of the cupcakes with colorful frosting.
12. Top each cupcake with white buttercream and gold sprinkles.
13. Place chocolate hats on top and serve.

95. Lemon Cheesecake with Vanilla Wafer

Serving Size: 16
Prep time: 10 minutes
Total Prep time: 50 minutes

Ingredients:

For the crust
- 1 ½ cups vanilla wafer crumbs
- ¼ cup plus 1 Tbsp. unsalted butter, melted
- 2 Tbsp. granulated sugar

For the filling
- 2 (8-ounce) packages of cream cheese
- 1 cup granulated sugar
- 1 cup sour cream
- Three egg, room temperature
- 1 tsp. vanilla extract
- 1 tsp. lemon extract
- 2 Tbsp. lemon juice
- Zest of 1 lemon

Instructions:
1. Heat the oven to 325 F.
2. Butter an 8-inch springform pan.
3. Cover the springform with a foil sheet from the outside.
4. Combine cookie crumbs with sugar and butter in a bowl.
5. Pour this mixture into the pan and press it firmly against the bottom.

6. Preparing the Filling:
7. Blend cream with sugar and cream cheese until smooth.
8. Stir in vanilla, sour cream, lemon extract, lemon zest, and juice.
9. Mix well at medium-high speed.
10. Gradually whisk in eggs while blending the mixture.
11. Pour this filling into the crust.
12. Bake for 50 minutes.
13. Allow it to cool for 1 hour.
14. Slice and serve.

96. Treacle Tart with Rosemary and Lemon

Serving Size: 12
Prep time: 10 minutes
Total Prep time: 50 minutes

Ingredients:

For the tart base
- 1 cup plain flour
- ¾ stick butter
- pinch of salt
- 2-3 Tbsp. cold water

For the filling
- ¼ stick butter
- zest and juice of half a lemon
- ⅔ cup + 1Tbsp. Lyle's Golden Corn Syrup

- 1 tsp. finely chopped rosemary
- 1 + ¼ cups fresh breadcrumbs
- ⅔ cup almond meal
- One egg

Instructions:
1. Set your oven to 375°F. Grease a cake pan.
2. Blend flour with butter in a blender until crumbly.
3. Gradually add water to the flour and mix to form a soft dough.
4. Press the dough in the baking dish and bake for 30 minutes until golden brown.
5. Meanwhile, melt butter in a medium saucepan until it turns brown.
6. Stir in all the remaining ingredients for filling except the egg.
7. Whisk well and cook on low heat until well mixed.
8. Whisk in egg and divide the mixture into the baked base.
9. Bake for another 20 minutes.
10. Allow it cool for 15 minutes, then slice and serve.

97. Chocolate Monster Cookies

Time: 2 hours
Servings: 6

Ingredients:
- 240 g (1 Cup) Dark chocolate
- 200 g (7 oz) Milk cholocate
- 120 g (4 oz) Butter
- 150 g (5 oz) flour

- 5 g (1 tsp) Baking powder
- One pinch of Coarse salt
- 2 Eggs 1Yolks
- 150 g (5 oz) Sugar
- 1 Vanilla bean
- Smarties Candy Eyes

Instructions:

1. Melt the 240 g of dark chocolate in a water bath and let it cool.
2. In the meantime, cut the butter into cubes and let it soften at room temperature, then add the sugar and the seeds of the vanilla bean and mix with a blender until a light and creamy mixture is obtained. Add the eggs and, in the meantime, mix. Finally, add the salt and the melted chocolate, now lukewarm.
3. At this point, add the sifted flour, the baking powder, and the milk chocolate, cut into small cubes.
4. Mix all the ingredients and then place the mixture in spoonfuls on a baking tray lined with parchment paper. Cover the cookies with Smarties and Candy Eyes.
5. Preheat the oven and bake at 360 degrees F for 15-20 minutes.
6. Remove the biscuits and place them on a wire rack to cool.

98. Butterbeer Krispy treats

Prep time: 15 minutes
Servings: 20

Ingredients:
- 2 ½ ounces butter, divided
- 15 ounces mini marshmallows
- 2 ½ ounces butterscotch dessert topping
- 48 ounces Rice Krispies cereal
- 8 ounces white chocolate chips
- 8 ounces butterscotch chips

Instructions:
1. Grease a 9x13-inch baking pan with ½ ounce of butter and set aside
2. In a microwavable bowl, melt 2 ounces of butter in the microwave and pour into a bigger bowl. Place marshmallows on top of the melted butter, then add butterscotch topping. Mix to coat marshmallows.
3. Heat butter-marshmallow mixture in the microwave for 30 seconds, remove and stir. Do this again in 30-second intervals until marshmallows have melted completely.
4. Pour Rice Krispies into the melted marshmallows and stir until coated.
5. Transfer cereal mixture to the baking pan and press down to distribute evenly. Cover pan with foil and chill for 2 hours.
6. Cut cereal treats into squares in the pan and places them on a piece of wax paper upside down.
7. Melt white chocolate and butterscotch chips in a microwaveable bowl in 30-second intervals until melted completed. Stir in between each interval.

8. Dip the bottom of each Rice Krispies square in the melted chocolate mixture and then place upside down on the wax paper. Cool completely before serving.

99. Butterbeer Latte

Cooking Time: 10 minutes
Servings: 8

Ingredients:
- 3 cups cream soda
- 4 cups whole milk
- ½ cup hot, brewed espresso
- ½ cup butter
- ½ cup brown sugar
- ½ cup butterscotch ice cream topping
- 4 tbsp powdered sugar
- ½ tsp vanilla extract
- 1 cup heavy cream

Instructions:
1. In a large mixing pot, whisk the heavy cream with the powdered sugar until the peaks are stiff. Add the vanilla extract, mix and then fold in the butterscotch ice cream topping. Set aside
2. Place the whole milk, butter, and brown sugar in a small saucepot. Heat over medium heat until simmering.
3. Take out the milk from the heat and add the cream soda and brewed espresso, stirring gently and then pouring into mugs.

4. Top with the butterscotch whipped cream and serve.

100. Healthy butterbeer smoothie

Prep time: 5 minutes
Servings: 1

Ingredients:
Vegan Caramel Sauce
- 8 ounces dates
- 2 ounces roasted cashews
- 8 ounces almond milk
- ¼ ounce vanilla extract
- ¼ teaspoon sea salt

Butterbeer Smoothie
- 2 ½ ounces almond milk
- ½ large frozen banana
- ¾ teaspoon vanilla
- 1/16 teaspoon ground cinnamon
- 1-ounce vegan caramel sauce
- Two ice cubes

Instructions:

Vegan Caramel Sauce
1. Put dates and roasted cashews in a large jar and cover with 8 ounces of hot water. Let them sit overnight to soften. Drain.

2. Combine all-vegan caramel sauce Ingredients in a blender and process until smooth. Chill until ready to use.

Butterbeer Smoothie
1. Mix all Ingredients for butterbeer smoothie in a blender and process until well combined and smooth.
2. Pour 1 ounce of caramel sauce down the sides of a tall glass and pour in butterbeer smoothie.

CONCLUSION

It's a great book with some very simple recipes, and it's enjoyable to read because it has some very awesome stories about Harry Potter. Give it a shot if you want to get those tasty meals.

This is an enjoyable book to use because Harry Potter is a very cool character that you never get tired of reading about him. Moreover, this book teaches you so much about cooking, all kinds of cooking tricks and cooking tips.

We hope we've been able to please you. You don't need to meet your long-time friends now if you want to eat these meals. All have been conjured up for you and you alone. You just have to decide which of the recipes you want to prepare.

So, the next time you want to revisit the wizarding world, you have this recipe book along with the movies and books.

We hope you will enjoy our yummy recipes if you are a true fan of Harry Potter. Let your imagination loose while trying these recipes, and you will find yourself somewhere in Hogwarts castle or Hogwarts Express!